15

CHARACTERISTICS
OF EFFECTIVE
PASTORS

GRACE AND GROWTH

LOVE FOR GOD

SPIRITUAL FORMATION

PERSONAL INTEGRITY

LOVE FOR THE CHURCH

SERVANT LEADER

MODEL OF HOLINESS

PRAYER LIFE

HOLY SPIRIT EMPOWERMENT

INSPIRED PREACHING

SURE CALLING

GODLY CHARACTER

PERSONAL ACCOUNTABILITY

STRONG MARRIAGE

VISIONARY LEADERSHIP

15

CHARACTERISTICS
OF EFFECTIVE
PASTORS

*How to Strengthen Your Inner Core
and Ministry Impact*

kevin w. mannoia
& larry walkemeyer

Regal

From Gospel Light
Ventura, California, U.S.A.

Published by Regal Books
From Gospel Light
Ventura, California, U.S.A.

Library of Congress Cataloging-in-Publication Data
Mannoia, Kevin W.
15 characteristics of effective pastors / Kevin W. Mannoia and Larry Walkemeyer.
p. cm.
ISBN 978-0-8307-4478-7 (hard cover) — ISBN 978-0-8307-4477-0 (international trade paper)
1. Pastoral theology. I. Walkemeyer, Larry. II. Title. III. Title: Fifteen characteristics of effective pastors.
BV4011.3.M36 2007
253'.2—dc22
2007000915

1 2 3 4 5 6 7 8 9 10 / 10 09 08 07

Rights for publishing this book in other languages are contracted by Gospel Light Worldwide, the international nonprofit ministry of Gospel Light. Gospel Light Worldwide also provides publishing and technical assistance to international publishers dedicated to producing Sunday School and Vacation Bible School curricula and books in the languages of the world. For additional information, visit www.gospellightworldwide.org; write to Gospel Light Worldwide, P.O. Box 3875, Ventura, CA 93006; or send an e-mail to info@gospellightworldwide.org.

Dedicated to
pastors and pastors to come
who pursue effectiveness
in their calling to build the Church to the glory of God.

CONTENTS

ACKNOWLEDGMENTS

This project has spanned many years. Through the process, many folks have impacted the outcome—to say that we are the only ones to have made this book a reality would be misguided.

As you can imagine, it is very difficult to list everyone who has touched the effort. If it isn't the space that would limit it, it's the memory! You might think that two minds could remember better than one, but the reality is that two authors just increase the number of folks to whom we owe a debt of gratitude.

There are some people, however, that we want to recognize for their involvement. Without them, there would be no book.

First and foremost, we are deeply grateful to each of the nine panelists for their patience and willingness to participate. They engaged in a long process and provided the basis for everything contained in these pages. These are folks who possess deep wisdom, broad experience and wonderful insight, and the characteristics themselves are the result of their gracious participation. You'd go a long way to hear just one of them in a conference, and here you get their *collective* insight and wisdom! Thank you to each of them.

John Burke
Maxie Dunnam
Jack Hayford
Walter Kaiser
H. B. London
Stephen Macchia
Gordon MacDonald
Jesse Miranda
Brenda Young

Even as we write this list, we are awed at the depth of understanding they represent and grateful for their love for pastors.

In addition, we are deeply grateful to the tremendous people who assisted us in identifying these panelists. They helped to ensure that the pastors who comprised the panel were truly ones to listen to.

Thanks to Michelle Price, who was ever-faithful in following up on the panelists, putting together the mailings and doing the hard office work of the survey logistics.

Chief among those deserving thanks are the members of the Walkemeyer and Mannoia families. For affirmation, support and loving encouragement, thanks to our children—Lindsey Walkemeyer and Kristyn, Christopher and Corey Mannoia—and especially to our wives, Deb and Kathy. We love you.

Regal Books deserves a huge thank-you for seeing the possibilities of this project and taking the risk. We are honored to be part of the Regal family, and we deeply appreciate the faith they have shown in us.

What a blessing to convey to you, the reader, our thanks for venturing into this book with faith that God will give you fresh insight for effectiveness in ministry.

And we humbly thank our God for the grace and confidence to allow these thoughts to flow.

All we are, we owe to You, Lord,
and all we have, we surrender to You.
For Your glory and for Your Church, we give ourselves afresh.
Thank You.

Kevin W. Mannoia
Larry Walkemeyer

WHAT MAKES AN EFFECTIVE PASTOR?

Have you ever wondered how often you're the topic of conversation in the parking lot? How good a job you're doing? How effective you are? It may make you shudder to think that people chat about you behind your back, but at least you and your church are important enough to bother talking about! Folks are interested in the Church and in effective leadership to further its mission.

Effective pastoral ministry flows from a complex integration of calling, character and competence, contextualized for Kingdom growth in the local community. Our greatest dream is for every pastor to pursue God with surrender and vulnerability to the Spirit's shaping so that his or her effectiveness will grow. Pastoral effectiveness translates into healthy, growing churches. To help pastors in the pursuit of effectiveness, we decided to find out what effectiveness looks like. We hoped that in providing some handholds, the climb to greater effectiveness might not be so daunting.

As we planned to address the question, we knew that adding our voices to the already myriad opinions on the subject might only confuse matters, so we set out to gain a consensus among a group of recognized pastoral experts. That way, we could craft a picture of pastoral effectiveness in concert with a qualified panel by drawing on their collective wisdom.

As times change, so the Church must change. For that to happen, leaders—specifically pastors—must grow, learn, develop and stretch to greater effectiveness. However, the mixed results of health and growth among local churches are indicators that this is not occurring.

A few years ago, the Association of Theological Schools began a project to study how to strengthen the connection between seminary education and the needs of churches. At the root of the project is a belief that a chasm is developing between our academic institutions and the Church: The way we train pastors and leaders is less and less relevant to meeting the needs of the churches to which we deploy them. The question driving the project is, How can we close the widening gap between theological education and the needs of the local church?

Underscoring the gap between seminary success and pastoral effectiveness is the growing proliferation of local church training institutes. As some churches have grown to mega-size, they have begun to train their own pastors, responding to the ineffectiveness they perceive in seminary-prepared leaders. This response may cause a celebration among church leaders who feel that the Church should be providing training based solely on the practical and functional needs of the current context, but the flaw in such thinking is that wells must be dug deep to have an ongoing supply of fresh water: The highly pragmatic leaders coming from these vocational institutes often find themselves in need of a deeper well. They yearn for broader knowledge into which their practical activities can fit and out of which their ministries can be propelled. The discipline of the mind, the pursuit of truth and a hunger for spiritual formation eventually call them to reconsider the effectiveness of purely functional training.

Portraits of Ineffectiveness

Nathan was a really nice man. He was in his early 60s and had been in ministry for decades. His children loved the Lord, and if anyone ever needed a caring shoulder to cry on, his was the best. He had been pastoring a small church in Orange County for nearly five years. The people loved him. He loved the people. But the growth of the church was simply not happening—it was shrinking in all categories. Some of the folks started to be concerned that the church may become extinct.

After spending a lot of time with Nathan, meeting with his board and being at the church, it became evident to me what had to happen: Nathan had to go. It sounds harsh, but that was the only way for the church to have a fighting chance for a future.

Nathan is a perfect example of a godly pastor who was simply not competent to lead that church in effective, healthy ministry. Acknowledging his incompetence is not an indictment of his character or a commentary about his identity as a pastor—he is a grace-filled, godly person. (And, thankfully, his godliness helped him to deal graciously with the decision to make a change in the pastoral leadership of that church.)

Beginning with that tough decision and followed by a few others, that Orange County church is now a thriving, healthy congregation that regularly sees people come to faith in Christ. It is many times larger than before and is impacting its community. People are regularly discipled into leadership and sent out to plant new churches. To effectively lead a church, it's not enough to be godly. Competence is required as well.

* * *

Stuart was the hope of his seminary class. He had all the signs of being a star. He was charismatic, good-looking, talented, a great communicator—and he had vision. Stuart had good grades in seminary and was praised by professors as a rare find in leadership. As he neared graduation, he was actively courted by district leaders and offered churches all over the country. Everybody knew that Stuart was going places. Everything he touched turned to gold.

Stuart settled on a small church of about 35 people. Growth would obviously be a challenge, but the church was in a highly desirable part of the country and had good facilities. Within a few short years, the church was bursting at the seams with 950 people attending three services. Overseas ministry tours took Stuart out regularly as his reputation grew. He made all the right decisions, hired all the right staff and was the picture-perfect image of ministry achievement. Pastors flew from across the country to learn the keys to his success, and Stuart demurely fielded questions about how they could do the same thing in their towns.

Yet life for that church forever changed when the district leader received a phone call reporting that Stuart was involved in an inappropriate relationship. Stuart's ordination was suspended. Something was seriously wrong in the foundation of his character, and when that flaw was exposed, the whole house of cards came crashing down. The church has since recovered its health, but the scars are still apparent: Broken trust, betrayal, hurt and pain scatter the landscape.

Stuart was an extremely competent leader. He had the skills. He was successful at building the institution. But in order to effectively lead a church, it's not enough to be competent. Godly character is required as well.

Effectiveness: What Is It?

In describing effectiveness, it is easy to be held hostage by one perspective or definition directly tied to the observable success of a local church. If a church does well in terms of bodies, budgets and buildings, then the pastor *must* be effective! If the pastor is loved and respected as wise by the parishioners, then the pastor *must* be effective! Either extreme is a trap: One leads to false success, the other to rationalized failure.

Effectiveness in pastoral ministry can be defined as *a careful integration of competence and godliness in the life of one who is called by God to lead in the Church.* Godliness in leadership involves matters of character and formation. Godly leaders are well-formed in their identity in Christ. They exhibit keen self-awareness that recognizes the dynamic and integral relationship between *who they are* and *what they do.* If there is a breakdown or inconsistency between these two elements, godly leaders notice it quickly and move to address the gap. These leaders see their identity and calling as a servant of God, reflecting Christ and extending the work of God in the world.

Competence in leadership involves matters of performance and outcomes. Competent leaders are gifted and talented and are also position-aware—in other words, they see clearly the impact their presence and leadership have on a church. They know when they are having a good impact, a bad effect or none at all, and they are usually the first ones to recognize when they should move on. Because of this keen impact-awareness, competent leaders are usually well deployed: They don't allow themselves to be placed in positions where they will get frustrated or hurt the church.

Although it is tempting to conclude that someone is effective based on the measurable results in the local church, doing so sells the soul of pastoral ministry to the merchants of success. Pastors often fall prey to this trap. The questions at many pastors' conferences point to the unspoken values lurking beneath the surface: "How big is your church?" or "What's your budget?" or "What's your salary?" Even our systems of reporting and accountability often fuel this misunderstanding of health and effectiveness. On one hand, pastors are told to develop healthy disciples in their congregations, and on the other, they are sent quarterly reports tallying conversions, baptisms, attendance, budget, debt, membership and quotas. Is it any wonder that the latter become the definition of success and pastoral effectiveness? After all, we expect what we regularly inspect.

Conversely, dismissing important signs that growth is lacking in the local Body of Christ is equally misguided. Often when a pastor comes face to face with the reality that his or her leadership is failing to meet his or her own expectations or those of the overseers or peer pastors, the "dance" begins. It goes something like this:

"Well, we didn't see anybody come to Christ, but the ones already committed are really going deep."

"We haven't grown numerically, but we're growing internally."

"No leaders have been developed, but someone has to minister to the followers."

"We've had no splits or divisions and our people are really connected."

"We haven't declined, so we're healthy."

Really?

Some people write books expressing their absolute conviction that pastoral effectiveness should be measured by the success or decline of the local church. Others decry any such "measurement" and argue that just being a healthy person will naturally result in effectiveness as a leader and in health as a church. And everyone is sure his or her opinion is right!

Well, so are we. The difference is that we have not started with assumptions about effectiveness in pastoral leadership. We have not presumed to define what effectiveness is and then tried to substantiate that definition with our personal opinions. We have simply asked the question, What are the characteristics of effective pastors? and allowed the consensual input of wise minds to give us the answer. As we call pastors to heightened effectiveness, we do so with a panel of experts who bring broad experience from a variety of ministry settings, all driven by their common Kingdom call.

You might say, "Yes, but who said they're the experts?" Great question. Actually, *you did*. Well, maybe not you specifically, but pastors like you from across the U.S. Between six and eight pastors in six different regions were asked who they perceive as a pastoral expert, to whom they would look for help in understanding the pastoral call. The results produced our panel of nine experts, who together developed the 15 Characteristics of Effective Pastors. (See appendix B for a description of the process used to develop and validate the 15 Characteristics.)

The result demonstrates that effectiveness is not confined to the categories of competent skills any more than it is limited to the qualities of godliness. Both of these dimensions are integral to effectiveness in pastors. Further, it is evident that effectiveness is not directly tied to the outcomes of the local church. Effective pastoral leadership may be present even when statistics do not show empirical success, just as effectiveness is not necessarily present just because the statistics are strong.

Effectiveness has an elusive quality of synergy that may only be explained in the economy of the Kingdom. It is more than the godliness of character in a person's nature. It is more than the brilliance of a person's leadership skills. It is more than the statistical outcomes of the local church. Effectiveness is all of these and more, intricately woven together in the life of one who is called by God.

We do not ask you to accept a tidy definition of pastoral effectiveness. The most *we* can do is identify characteristics that our experts agree are the markers of effectiveness in pastors—ultimately, it is God who defines and evaluates our effectiveness.

*   *   *

God's Word and Church history provide our foundation for an accurate understanding of what an effective pastor actually is. A survey of Scripture reveals that there is no explicit definition of the characteristics of effective pastors. There is, however, insight into the character and mission of *faithful* pastors. Scripture also paints a clear picture of ineffective and even deceptive pastors. An overview of some of these passages can center our thinking on God's idea of effectiveness.

In addition to Scripture, foundations of pastoral effectiveness have been shaped and guided by Church tradition, which informs our understanding today. A few godly leaders in particular are examples of this dynamic influence. You'll find brief snapshots of some important biblical passages and historic Church leaders on the page between each characteristic—let these examples be lights on your path toward effective pastoring.

Leadership is a stewardship issue. Allowing the character Christ is building within us to find expression in our talents, gifts and passions is an act of stewarding the trust that God has placed in us.

Peter Drucker describes the difference between efficiency and effectiveness in terms of activities: Efficiency is doing things right, while *effectiveness is doing the right things.* It's a nice contrast that reminds us of the value of strategic leadership, yet even this clever turn of phrase does not fully capture the nature of effectiveness in pastoral ministry. Pastoral effectiveness is much more than "doing things," even if they are the right things done right. Effectiveness in the economy of the kingdom of God is as much about *identity* as it is about *activities.* Who we are is as important as what we do. Bringing these elements together in careful integration and spiritual synergy is at the root of effective leadership in the Church.

As you unpack your thinking about the 15 Characteristics, please remember that they are not to be used as a checklist—*they are descriptive.* It's the Holy Spirit who shapes our lives as we pursue Christ, and it's only as we give ourselves in humility and vulnerability to Him that the characteristics become the natural consequence.

Pursue Christ first. With all your life, submit yourself to the ongoing work of the Holy Spirit to mold you in Christlikeness. Be cognizant of your condition and your deficiencies, but in the face of ineffectiveness, don't take into your own hands the task reserved for God: *forming you.* Lean with all your might into effectiveness, but remember that it starts with pursuing God, who shapes the characteristics in you for the good of the Kingdom.

GRACE AND GROWTH: *Humility?*

Possesses a lively experience of God's grace and growth in his or her Christian walk

A grande, extra-hot soy latte almost always hits me right where I need it. I think I'm more open to the Holy Spirit if I include a latte in my morning devotions—the Holy Spirit is my helper, but He seems to be helped by caffeine.

I admit that I don't understand people who willingly choose caffeine-free coffee. They are like doctors who smoke, firefighters who let their kids play with matches or Boeing employees who are afraid to fly. There is an incongruence that raises suspicions in my mind.

My friend says, "I love coffee. I love the smell of coffee, the taste of coffee, the warmth of coffee," but he takes it decaf because "I can do without the jolt." I needle him about missing the power of the bean and the blessing of all those antioxidants. (I'm not an addict, but I do enjoy the buzz!) He's missing the real thing—he's not having a lively experience of what a latte really *is*.

Effective pastors have a lively experience of God's grace and growth in their Christian walk. They refuse decaf Christianity. The Christian clichés, tastes, smells, songs and symbols of success aren't enough for them. They aren't happy without the kick, the jolt, the buzz of true grace. They have an ever-increasing realization of their personal need for the daily grace of God in their own lives, and this need motivates them to continually seek personal spiritual development.

Giving your life today for a faded memory in the scrapbook of your past is neither compelling nor authentic. Communicating a reality that has been learned from a book—or only been *real* to someone else—is decaffeinated grace. The power of effective ministry is the integrity of the interaction between the messenger and the message. Is grace fresh in the life of the one proclaiming grace to the world? Is the salvation being preached saving the messenger today?

Experiencing God's grace is like a kaleidoscope. You look through and see a colorful display of beauty, then you shake it up or turn it and the same ingredients create an entirely new, colorful portrait. In pastoral ministry, grace is multifaceted and shares its light in various ways: We live in and depend on the grace of truth, of salvation, of God's forgiveness, of God's favor, of God's presence, of God's blessing, of God's help.

It is easy to reduce grace to a theological concept, but a life consumed by grace is vibrant and powerful for ministry. Grace must be experienced, not as an abstract notion, but as the currency of the Kingdom that enlivens your journey with God. There are five big ideas that are central to a lively experience of God's grace in pastoral ministry.

1. The Grace of Credibility

Effective pastors, while cherishing the affirmation of the Church and the preparation of studies, view their most important ministry credentials as the vitality of grace in their own lives. An awareness of grace starts, sustains and shapes the entire course of ministry—this sense of need and dependency on God is the posture a pastor must assume and maintain.

Grace is as necessary to a pastor as the clothes he wears. Many pastors I have spoken with have a common bad dream in which they stand up in the pulpit to preach and suddenly realize that they are clad only in their underwear. The expressions of shock from their parishioners

Sometimes Grace leaves me because of my Cynical Sarcastic take on life, Church, + ministry.

make it obvious that their near-nakedness has not gone unnoticed!

Without a lively experience of grace, this nightmare is, in effect, real. Many times, the experience of grace is peeled away so gradually that it goes undetected, and the effectiveness of ministry incrementally declines until a moment of stark reality hits: "I'm powerless. I'm naked. I'm ineffective." Painful though the realization is, at least the problem has been recognized and that pastor can set out to be changed—the unfortunate ones are those who never realize that vibrant grace has gone. They go through the motions while locked in the trap of ineffectiveness.

The first description of the relationship between young Jesus and His Father paints this picture of the maturing credibility of grace: "And the child grew and became strong; he was filled with wisdom, and the grace of God was upon him" (Luke 2:40). Jesus is described two decades later as one who was "full of grace and truth" (John 1:14).

The first apostles carried this mantle of grace forward: "With great power the apostles continued to testify to the resurrection of the Lord Jesus, and much grace was upon them all" (Acts 4:33). Stephen was described as "a man full of God's grace and power, [who] did great wonders and miraculous signs among the people" (Acts 6:8). Paul inextricably linked grace and his ministry call: "Through him and for his name's sake, we received grace and apostleship to call people from among all the Gentiles to the obedience that comes from faith" (Rom. 1:5).

The most effective minister in the history of the gospel drew his credibility from grace alone! Paul introduced himself like this: "Here is a trustworthy saying that deserves full acceptance: Christ Jesus came into the world to save sinners—of whom I am the worst. But for that very reason I was shown mercy so that in me, the worst of sinners, Christ Jesus might display his unlimited patience as an example for those who would believe on him and receive eternal life" (1 Tim. 1:15-16). If Paul had been a songwriter, he would have beaten John Newton to the copyright of "Amazing Grace." It was grace that saved a wretch like him, that taught his heart to fear, that delivered him from his fears, and that brought him through dangers, toils and snares. Grace saved him. Grace chose him. Grace restored him. Grace empowered him. Grace kept him. Grace—the undeserved kindness and presence of God—did this for Paul. His life was caffeinated with grace.

Ministering from a position shaped by the reception of radical grace imparts a distinctive and undeniable flavor to the pastorate. It humbles the messenger. It simplifies the message. It emboldens the delivery. In this fatiguing day of celebrity preachers, stadium-sized mega-churches, prolific academicians and comparison-shopping churchgoers, it's invigorating to return to the simplicity of grace alone, through faith alone, in Christ alone. That's the résumé that really counts. Degrees can be earned and ordination can be achieved, but grace can only be believed and received.

God's distribution of grace is unconditional and constant, but our reception is selective and sporadic. Our personal reception of grace must be renewed daily. Fresh grace stimulates the gratitude and wonder that empower us to share truth with authenticity, to share grace from the freshness of our own experience. We can credibly communicate amazing grace only when we have been recently awed by it.

To keep the bad dream from coming true, pastors must keep the robe of grace by the front door of our lives. Without it, we *should* be embarrassed to go into public. When pastors are dressed only in the emperor's new clothes, it's no wonder ministry is a nightmare.

2. The Grace of Cleansing

A profound sense of gratitude for the grace of the cross drives the effective pastor, reverberating from a heart acutely aware of what God has rescued us *from*: "Where I was" and "Where I might have been." The well-worn story of D. L. Moody's seeing the bum in the gutter should still resonate in the mind of every pastor. When someone insulted the drunk, Moody pronounced with deep feeling, "But for the grace of God, there go I."

Growing up in a Christian home and a squeaky-clean family left little sense of awe in me for the greatness of God's grace. God's law was my friend because I could trust it to be predictable and reward me for good behavior. It wasn't until my 20s (after some sinful detours) that the grace of the cross became caffeinated for me. "All other ground is sinking sand" was a reality, not just a Sunday School song. My whole world had become a sand pit—there was no safe place to stand, except under the cross.

Living in that place of despair and discovery, I prayed, "Make it real and make it last . . . don't ever allow any other place on Earth to feel safe, satisfying or solid." With only a few spiritual speed bumps, that prayer has been answered. The grace of the cross moves me deeply because I know I need it desperately. It picks me up daily when I fall. Engagement with grace allows me to talk about it with the authenticity of personal experience.

It is this grace that cleanses a pastor from her weekly failures and empowers her to stand once more in the holiness of the pulpit. Standing there on the merits of her own good behavior is folly—good behavior can earn gold stars in Sunday School, but it's woefully incapable to gain God's power for the pulpit. That job is reserved for the cross.

The cross must be the pivot point for the effective pastor, the place around which the rest of life and ministry revolves. In junior high basketball, Coach taught us how to keep the pivot foot planted. He barked, "Gentlemen, you can move in any direction you want as long as you don't move that foot!" Ministry may take us in hundreds of directions, but grace keeps our foot planted on the cross.

Think Grace First !!

When grace is freshly received in your life, it becomes your natural response to the needs and sins of others. An effective pastor doesn't dispense legalistic solutions to the convoluted problems of people—instead, he offers the same grace he's living in. He lifts the eyes of the guilty to the mercy of the cross, and this grace-filled approach becomes a hallmark of his ministry. His own daily encounters with grace give him authority to hand it out freely.

3. The Grace of Renewal

Cynicism is an occupational hazard of the ministry. They should issue construction-grade hardhats to protect pastors from the debris of falling commitments:

- The energetic newcomer who promised a year ago to revitalize the children's ministry, who is now helping the local mega-church's "Love-a-Kid-Land" become the talk of the town
- The millionaire businessman who puts his arm around you and says, "Pastor, we'll fix this place up," but who really means, "I will pay for it if you do it my way"
- The prayer warrior who takes your secrets to God, and then to the congregation
- The dynamic couple that teaches your young-married group until you discover he's having an affair

Hardening our hearts against the rubble of broken promises may seem like the only survival strategy, but the luxury of cynicism comes at a price no pastor can afford. Experiencing God's grace in supportive and sustaining ways is the healthy alternative. God's grace repairs the ragged edges of a heart worn out by disappointment and renews the fatigued soul that argues against carrying one more burden.

It's not just the broken promises of other people that are disillu-sioning—pastors can't live up to our own vows! Almost every set of ordination vows includes statements that, despite our best efforts, we fail miserably to keep. The shortcomings of pastors can quickly become the fuel the enemy uses to burn us out. The ugly reality of impatience or selfishness or gluttony appearing on Saturday evening is like a bad pimple the night before the prom: It makes you want to cancel your date on Sunday.

Grace is no less sufficient for the pastor than for the parishioner. While there are certainly patterns of conduct that should disqualify a pastor from his position, most pastors need to preach their sermons of grace to themselves. Grace qualifies a pastor to stand up after a week of failures and boldly declare the gospel. If a minimum degree of righteousness were a prerequisite to preaching on Sundays, pulpits would be silent. If we preach our own righteousness, we don't have an authorita-tive message, no matter how good we've been living. Paul made it clear in 2 Corinthians 4:5 that "we do not preach ourselves, but Jesus Christ as Lord." We come to the throne of grace to receive mercy in our time of need (see Heb. 4:16). Wise pastors run to the throne of grace when they sin instead of "pulling an Adam" by hiding from God. This ques-tion of where we go when we blow it is essential to answer rightly: If we avoid God or deny our sin or beat ourselves up or rationalize it away, we are in trouble. Embracing grace is the only safe response to sin.

When Paul was disappointed that God would not remove the thorn in his flesh, he heard the Lord speak to him in prayer. God's words were both disappointing and victorious: The problem wouldn't go away, but His grace was more than adequate to power him through it. Paul's response? "Therefore I will boast all the more gladly about my weak-nesses, so that Christ's power may rest on me" (2 Cor. 12:9).

The commercial that depicts "The Nestea Plunge" captures the refreshing nearness of grace. A hot, thirsty, sweaty person deposits a few coins in a vending machine. When a bottle of Nestea falls out, a pool of cool water appears in the background. As she drinks the tea, she freefalls backward with of huge splash of joy. What a compelling picture of grace! Just like the pool, grace appears without our effort—our part is to fall into it, enjoy it and be changed by it.

4. The Grace of Provision

God's grace makes available all the provisions we need at this place and time. Effective pastors depend on these resources and know that they are in trouble without them.

Grace brings God's presence to bear on the situation at hand. Paul emphasizes this in 2 Corinthians 9:8: "And God is able to make all grace abound to you, so that in all things at all times, having all that you need, you will abound in every good work." *All* grace, in *all* things, at *all* times, having *all* you need—this is the grace of provision.

Grace is powerfully put on display in the account of Elijah at Brook Kerith. After delivering a controversial sermon that his congregation despised, Elijah was told by God to head 15 miles into the desert (where many pastors wake up on Monday morning!). God's grace had prepared an unexpected retreat center for Elijah—the Pizza Hut delivery birds knew exactly where he was staying. With two grace-full deliveries a day, Elijah was provided for, restored and empowered for his next sermon.

Elijah was sent miles from the closest Starbucks, McDonalds or 7-Eleven. He was helpless unless help came from above, and it was obvious to him that he was in a place of utter dependence on God's grace. But often it's not as obvious to pastors that *we* are living at Brook Kerith, a place of pure reliance on God. After all, there are books, magazines, DVDs and seminars to fill us! The best sermons from the biggest preachers are only a click and a few bucks away! But confidence in other delivery systems can hinder the supply of grace. Both James and Peter declared that God opposes the proud but gives grace to the humble (see Jas. 4:6 and 1 Pet. 5:5). Any sense of self-sufficiency can block God's available grace.

We must constantly revisit the question, "Am I doing something *for* God or something *with* God?" Doing things *for* God places the emphasis on *me* and makes a hero out of *me*. It replaces the grace of God with my own works. Doing things *with* God, on the other hand, forces a dependence on God to supply direction for the mission and provisions to carry it out. It is from grace that the gifts of the Spirit flow. Paul reminds us that "we have different gifts, according to the grace given us" (Rom. 12:6). Through grace, we have every gift we need to carry out our unique mission.

5. The Grace of Growth

Our panel of experts was clear that Characteristic 1 was not only a reception of grace but also a *growing experience* of grace. The apostle Peter wrote that growth is not an optional accessory: "Grow in the grace and knowledge of our Lord and Savior Jesus Christ" (2 Pet. 3:18). The grace we have received is a gift to be expanded, developed and nurtured.

This ongoing experience of grace is like farming in a jungle: Grace makes a clearing, but if left to itself, the undergrowth of sin begins its insidious assault to overtake the cleared area. As the circumstances of life present new challenges, new dimensions of God's grace must be drawn on to make a larger clearing—or at least to cut a path through the forest! Grace's territory expands in our hearts as the exploration of life leads down previously un-traveled roads. Some new roads are cleared as an inescapable part of life—the loss of loved ones, illness, financial surprises. Others appear when we purposely venture into uncharted places to further God's mission. If we are living grace-dependent lives, we walk those new roads willingly in order to cultivate new growth in our lives.

When my wife was suddenly diagnosed with a rare and aggressive form of cancer, I was initially stunned into a numbness of soul. Then, waves of dread broke over me—my wisdom and training were unable to keep me afloat. The grace I had sailed in up to that point was inadequate for the new sea of fears, but as our church prayed and as I begged God to give me a new "life boat" of grace, God did exactly that: I was in dark waters, bobbing around with waves crashing over my head, yet I was dry and unsinkable.

Pastors have a tendency to plateau in their spiritual development. We start repeating the same year over and over, rather than living a new year with God. We get comfortable with our weaknesses and call a truce with our sin problems. The grace of growth, however, demands self-revelation. Grace reveals my sin, immaturity and unhealthy patterns of behavior, and then offers forgiveness and the power to change. As we appropriate grace, it begins to transform areas of immaturity.

I recently received a card for my birthday that showed some singing hippies from the 1960s on the front. I opened the card and it said, "Someone's aging, Lord, kum-ba-ya!" The question is not "Are we aging?" but "Are we *changing*?" To paraphrase Paul, are we putting away more childish ways or has our talking and thinking become stuck in some previous stage of development (see 1 Cor. 13:11)?

The wall of the Starbucks where I write has a conversation between two Greek sirens painted on it. The conversation ends with these words: "For it is only when they stop growing that humans become old." Nineteenth-century theologian and pastor Horace Bushnell made a similar observation: "Where growth stops, death begins."

Pastor Al is a friend who was a highly effective pastor. He is a hero in the circle of people who know him, and I am blessed to be in that circle. Al is heroic to me because of the life of grace he has lived and modeled. He has refused to grow old and has instead kept growing up. On his eightieth birthday, he went water skiing to celebrate! A couple years later, I saw Al early in the morning walking hand in hand with his bride of 60 years—they had walked several miles to have their devotions on Huntington Beach Pier.

The last time I caught up with Al, he was leading a group for young married couples—some as many as six decades his junior!—and had recently been visiting an emerging church near his home. At 82, Al was learning something new. The vitality of grace in Al's life twinkled in his eyes and sparkled in his smile. He still had dreams about how God would use the rest of his life. Someone once wrote, "A person is not old until their memories are more important than their dreams." Al's life reminds me of Acts 2:17, which promises dreams to the elderly.

Al's lively experience of grace and growth was not born out of the ease of a sedate or trouble-free ministry career. In fact, just the opposite is true: Church difficulties, board member challenges, staff meltdowns, numerical plateaus and personal health problems were all part of Al's life and ministry. But all of those were situations in which he embraced grace. His posture of placing grace as the pivot point of ministry was what allowed him to flourish while peers around him wilted.

Pastors confront the hardships of ministry with a mind-set of *escape, management* or *growth*. The first reaction is to escape, to run from the problem lest the pain increase. Conflict avoidance might seem the safest path to travel, but it is a road to nowhere. Growth never happens on the path of no resistance—that's like working out by sitting in the recliner with a bag of chips! It feels good, but it's completely counter-productive.

The second response is to manage the difficulty, holding it at a distance to avoid getting close to the mess. With this option, a pastor keeps his heart from engaging with pain, disappointment or betrayal. Refusing to engage authentically with the emotions of the problem keeps him from the possibility of growth. Grace can only reach as deep as his vulnerability, and stoically managing the difficulty keeps him on an unhealthy pedestal of being a pastor more than a person. Such a response demonstrates self-reliance instead of dependence on grace, and it drives an unhealthy wedge between a pastor and his church.

The third approach is to embrace the trial with the help of grace. A pastor allows the grace of God to assist her in putting her arms around the circumstance to feel the hurt, and steps down from the pastoral pedestal to be a student in the school of pain. She asks, "How is God dwelling in the midst of this? How is God's reign going to manifest itself as I stand and endure? How is God shaping the interior dimensions of my heart as I refuse to flee? How is God's grace going to show up here?"

Effective leaders look for new lessons that will keep them growing, that will stretch their hearts and minds to greater levels of maturity. They ask for the continual grace of growing up, not just growing older. The effective pastor is a learner much more than a teacher. If and when that priority reverses, a gradual decline begins into a "form of godliness but denying the power thereof" (2 Tim. 3:5, *KJV*). If the lessons that are prepared are not first delivered to the soul of the pastor, they are no longer gifts of grace but displays of arrogance. They are like the box of chocolates your brother got to first: The pretty wrappers are there, but the good stuff is missing.

Every well-known Christian leader who fails serves to remind us of the dangers of preaching grace to everyone but ourselves. That's what is known as "Destination: Deception." Destination: Deception happens when a pastor feels that he has arrived at an adequate place of spiritual maturity. He may even develop a sense of entitlement because he has sacrificed and worked hard for the Kingdom—God will surely overlook a few unholy pleasure trips! He may feel he has arrived at a level where he doesn't need to carefully apply what he preaches to others—all that's left to do is help others get to his high altitude of holiness. The deception that he has reached his destination lulls him into standing still.

Flying into Seattle-Tacoma airport was always a treat for me in my younger days. In the satellite concourse, there was a long escalator that was usually deserted, and I loved to run up the downward-moving escalator. It wasn't difficult to get to the top unless I stopped moving. If I stood still, I didn't keep my place—I lost ground. I was either moving up or being carried down.

Ministry is like running up the downward-moving escalator. It's not hard to move up until you start believing that you can stop growing and keep climbing. Grace is the favor of God that calls you higher, calls you forward into the person you can become.

Pastors living in grace are like crystal goblets: If it's the real thing, it sings when you rub your finger around the edges. Authenticity is proved by the song that arises when rubbed. Grace creates a life that sings when rubbed by the realities of ministry. Without grace, ministry can only be carried on and covered up by the efforts of a person playing pastor.

*   *   *

Fat-free half-and-half, sugarless ice cream, salt-free potato chips, veggie burgers, decaf coffee: They're all missing the ingredient that defines them. Unlike these meaningless substitutes, effective pastors authentically encounter the essential ministry ingredient of grace. Without it, ministry has no hope of delivering the jolt the world needs. Without it, ministry is empty of the ingredient that defines it.

Pastor, you are the leader God has called to keep grace ever-present in the health of your congregation, and it must be a lively experience in your own life if you are to be effective in bestowing it.

In Ezekiel 34, the Lord pronounces judgment on the shepherds of Israel. This judgment is because these shepherds "only take care of themselves" and do not "take care of the flock" (vv. 2-3). The specific charges are that they do not help the weak, sick or injured; they do not rescue strays and the lost; and they rule the flock harshly, benefiting themselves with the best the flock has to offer (see vv. 3-4). Because of these shortcomings, the sheep are scattered and the shepherds will be held accountable. The Lord will rescue the sheep, tend to them and care for the injured and weak (see vv. 11-12,16).

Conversely, effective shepherd-pastors fill a role of delegated authority, extensions of God's preeminent shepherding role. They place the sheep's welfare above their own as they care for the weak, sick, injured and lost. They keep their flocks from scattering by providing direction, administering correction and building unity. These shepherds blend selfless caring with clear leadership.

LOVE FOR GOD:

Possesses a deep, personal love for God

At 2 A.M. on a desolate stretch of I-40 in the desert of Arizona, the Lord whispered to me. Sixteen hours earlier I had climbed into my Jeep, put my fiancée's picture on the seat next to mine and sped off toward Los Angeles where she was waiting. My ardor for her was at its utmost intensity. That blonde beach girl had captured the heart of this Kansas farm boy. I had a new understanding of the concept of "passion," and my passion kept me from stopping except for mandatory reasons—filling up or emptying out.

Maybe the truck-stop hot dogs contributed to my revelation, but the Lord was undeniably talking: "How you feel about her is how I feel about you and how I want you to feel about Me!"

God loves using deserts and darkness to grip the attention of his servants. That night in the Arizona blackness at 70 miles per hour, I prayed an earnest prayer of commitment: "God, I receive Your passion for me. I choose to allow passion for You to be the primary mark of my life." Seeking to live out that prayer has dramatically shaped my ministry.

As a 20-year-old youth pastor eager to impact lives and leave my unique mark on the ministry world, a lack of enthusiasm was not my problem. The question was whether or not my zeal was correctly focused. Was my passion misdirected toward the possibilities of my ministry, the rightness of the cause of Christianity, the adventure of engaging the powers around me in a spiritual gunfight, an "I'll show them how to do it" bravado, or the pettiness of my own ego? Or was my passion focused first and foremost on the person of God, personal intimacy with my King and the privilege of revealing His beauty to the broken world around me?

God First Loves Us

God Wants me

Pastors who are truly effective discover and revel in God's passion for them. They prioritize the development of their personal love relationship with God. They see "ministry success" as a cheap imitation of what they really desire: a daily engagement of their heart with God. Our panel of experts rated Characteristic #2 highest for pastors who have ministries that are effective over the long term. Any pursuit that takes precedence over the development of this essential trait undermines a pastor's true effectiveness. Without a strong, deep and personal love for God, ministry is in constant danger of devolving into careerism, and ministry as a "job" hobbles the effectiveness of the pastor.

Love for God is the satisfaction and rest that every pastor craves. Somewhere in the deep and quiet recesses of the pastor's soul there is the conviction that no success, no raise, no denominational plaque or award can replace the absolute reality of relationship with God. For years I have told fresh-faced recruits entering the pastoral ranks, *Good* "Ministry must be the overflow of your personal love life with Jesus. If people are getting what God should be getting, then everyone's getting the short end of the stick."

Psalm 19 indicates that God conveys His presence to us through creation. Sunrises, flowers, a baby's laughter, the wagging tail of the dog, a favorite song on the radio, hot showers, tasty food, a spouse's hug, a cool breeze, sand between your toes, sun on your face . . . these can transcend their surface value and become whispers of God's love to us. God's passion is being communicated in countless ways, but unless we awaken, we will rush by these love notes as we wait for divine fireworks to blow us away.

Love Before Position

The effective pastor receives and then returns this love of God. He pursues and embraces deep and personal emotions for the Lord. The love relationship that the saints of old had with God captures his imagination and becomes his desire. King David's priority becomes his own: "One thing I ask of the LORD, this is what I seek: that I may dwell in the house of the LORD all the days of my life, to gaze upon the beauty of the LORD and to seek him in his temple" (Ps. 27:4).

Pastors who forget that they are sheep before they are shepherds will miss this passion that David understood and enjoyed. The psalmist king's dance of self-abandonment before the ark of God is a reminder for spiritual leaders not to allow their roles to be what defines them. David's wife Michal was appalled that the king would so easily forget his professional position and strike out in such a personally zealous display of worship, but David understood the joy and necessity of the presence of God in the city. His personal worship was of greater importance than maintaining his public persona.

A friend and his wife wanted to learn to dance, so they studied dance steps, memorized dance steps and practiced dance steps in the privacy of their own home, all without music. They were terrible, and they found the whole process absolutely boring. What saved them was their decision to take a risk and attend a dance with live music. Suddenly the lifeless steps they had learned took on new life! The spirit of the music turned their joyless lessons into passion for the dance floor.

Our love for God is always in danger of degenerating into dance lessons without the music. Our personal worship can be just as lifeless if we recite our Christian creeds without the music of the Spirit to create an interactive dance with God. The good news according to Zephaniah is that God delights in His children and rejoices over them with singing (see Zeph. 3). *He* provides the music! Our dance with God begins as we hear the music of His passion for us, not as we grit our teeth to perform our religious work of personal devotions.

Simon Tugwell reminds us, "So long as we imagine that it is we who have to look for God, we must often lose heart. But it is the other way around. He is looking for us."[1] John Wesley echoes this: "We must love God before we can be holy at all, this being the root of holiness. Now we cannot love God, till we know he loves us: We love him, because he first loved us."[2]

Elijah's ministry flowed from a place of deep love for God. God sent Elijah to a cave to listen. When it finally came, God's voice was a gentle whisper: "What are you doing here, Elijah?" Elijah answered from the core of his being: "I have been very zealous for the LORD God Almighty" (see 1 Kings 19:9-10). This zeal propelled Elijah's ministry.

Likewise, God's question to pastors is, "What are you doing here?" If the answer is not "I am very zealous for the LORD," then effectiveness and enjoyment in ministry is waning. Pastors must be driven by their passion for God. Jesus was including pastors when He said, "'Love the Lord your God with all your heart and with all your soul and with all your mind.' This is the first and greatest commandment" (Matt. 22:37-38). The greatness of following this command is demonstrated in multiple ways, including pastoral effectiveness—true greatness in ministry is directly linked to obeying it. There is no substitute or detour.

Ministering from Love

Following the resurrection, Peter and the other disciples were fishing. After some coaching from a stranger on the shore, the disciples hit the mother lode of fish—153 big ones. It was then that Peter recognized the stranger: It was Jesus! Forgetting the catch of a lifetime, Peter dove in to swim to his friend and Savior. You can visualize Peter dripping wet, wrapping Jesus in a big bear hug. The success of Peter's fishing trip could not substitute for being in the presence of Jesus, and neither can the size of a pastor's ministry replace the satisfaction of being in the presence of God.

After breakfast that morning, Jesus asked Peter, "Do you really love me?" and then explained that the outflow of Peter's love must be feeding His sheep. Loving the sheep begins in loving the Shepherd. Loving the people flows from a deep personal love for God.

Pastors are often caught up in an addiction to doing good things. They rush from a counseling appointment to a committee meeting to a hospital visit to writing encouraging e-mails to a long list of hurting folks. Rushing around doing good provides a temporary high, but—as with any addiction—the high is too temporary and too shallow to replace the real substance the pastor craves. If left unchecked, good can become a substitute for God. The rush will fade into a rationale that excuses the pastor from the priority of a personal interface with the living God.

John Wesley confronted this kind of rationalization by speaking earnestly to those who redefined love for God as good works: "But will this satisfy him who hungers after God? No . . . the knowledge of God in Christ Jesus; the life which is hid with Christ in God; the being joined unto the Lord in one spirit; the having fellowship with the Father and the Son; the walking in the light as God is in the light; the being purified even as He is pure—this is the religion, the righteousness, he thirsts after: Nor can he rest, till he thus rests in God."[3]

Until a pastor awakens to the passionate love of God that is daily pursuing him, he will suffer from relational anemia that saps his ministry energy. However, as a pastor lives in the consistent cascade of love flowing from the Father's heart, an unwavering source of spiritual

[handwritten marginal note:] Don't Be afraid to Express your Love for God's world. It is the Beginning of the end for Cynicism

power moves into action. This revelation of God's love translates ordinary occurrences into divine expressions of affection.

The sincerity and authenticity of the pastor is almost always sensed in some intuitive way by the people whom she or he is leading. People perceive whether actions are flowing from a love of ministry, a love of position, a love of self, or a deep love for God. People respect and willingly follow a pastor who clearly exudes a personal passion for God.

These are some practical results for ministry that spring from a deep, personal love for God:

1. The deeper and the more personal the love for God, the more resilient a pastor will be. The pastor who truly loves people exposes himself to rejection, misunderstanding, betrayal, disappointment and indifference as a part of the package. The pastor's bounce-back factor is directly linked to his ability to receive the healing love of God and to refill his emotional tank in God's loving presence.

2. Risk-taking is an essential part of effective ministry leadership. The safety net of an intimate relationship with God fuels the courage to "go for it" in daring ways.

3. Insecurity is often the hobgoblin that keeps pastors stuck in the ruts of the familiar and the ineffectiveness of the routine. The love of God secures the self-image of a pastor to reject cookie-cutter solutions and implement the strategies that reflect who she is as a leader.

4. Ineffectiveness is often the result of motives that are impure. This characteristic consistently draws pastors to examine their own hearts and realign themselves with the First Com-

mandment. Loving the Lord our God opens the door for the blessings that pastors desire.

* * *

Pastor Jack Hayford told a group of us that his day begins by getting from his back to his knees. He rolls out of bed and kneels with an open Bible before the Lord, and it's this priority on passion for God that feeds his ministry the rest of the day. Let his example remind us that our love for God spurs our pursuit of God. Ministry can be exhausting, and effectiveness is directly linked to a pastor's ability to successfully refresh his life. The pastor who has developed a private place of intimacy with the Lord, an ability to escape to His presence and be held in His love, is the pastor who will not faint, but grow stronger through the course of his ministry. The apostle John says that God is love (see 1 John 4). The foundational requirement of effectively ministering God's love is that we receive it and live immersed in it.

Isn't part of loving God loving his Word?
To know it is to know Him.
To know him is to love him Deeper.

Notes
1. Simon Tugwell, *Prayer Living with God* (Springfield, IL: Templegate Publishers, 1975), n.p.
2. John Wesley, *The Works of John Wesley* (Grand Rapids, MI: Zondervan Publishing House, 1972), p. 115; see also p. 127.
3. Ibid., p. 268.

FOUNDATIONS IN CHURCH HISTORY

JOHN WYCLIFFE (1320-1384)

John Wycliffe, the leading Oxford scholar of his day, summed up his thoughts on pastoral effectiveness when he said:

> There are two things which pertain to the status of pastor: the holiness of the pastor and the wholesomeness of his preaching. He ought to be holy, so strong in every virtue that he would rather desert every kind of human intercourse, all the temporal things of this world, even mortal life itself, before he would sinfully depart from the truth of Christ.

Wycliffe's understanding of the necessary depth of commitment a pastor must have to be effective might be intimidating, but if taken to heart, will be transformative both personally and in ministry for any pastor who lives by them.

SPIRITUAL FORMATION:

Develops regular habits for spiritual formation (devotions, fasting, solitude, and so forth)

Digging ditches is not my idea of a good time. It's hard work and time consuming, though once you get in shape, there can be a genuine delight and satisfaction in the digging process. Still, ditches aren't an end to themselves—they're not works of art. They are works of preparation. Ditches are dug to contain or channel the real treasure—the water that will flow through them.

Having dug many ditches in my day, I can attest to the fact that there is no science to it. Every ditch digger has to find the method that works for him. The principles of ditch digging are simple: If you do the work, the water will flow where it does the most good and accomplishes its purpose. The ditch, though important, will be mostly forgotten. The same is true for developing regular habits that allow for spiritual formation.

Effective pastors recognize their brokenness and consequent need to prepare their souls for the presence of the Holy Spirit through spiritual habits. This vigorous life of spiritual discipline toughens and softens the soul so that daily life is lived from a spiritual center. Every pastor must dig ditches that provide a path for God to fill his or her life, and spiritual disciplines are the primary means for spiritual formation to take place. These disciplines are practices of physical and mental action that give God access to our hearts so that we are shaped to live more like Jesus.

While these disciplines constitute the basis of your spiritual formation, there may be other habits unique to you that are important as well. Perhaps, for example, you make a habit of having dinner with your family or breakfast with your spouse, or you take a monthly trip to a park or beach (not to pray, just to admire!). These habits, too, can unlock our hearts for God to enter in.

Elisha's Ditches

Scripture contains an illustration of the power of a ditch. In a conflict with Moab, the Israelite army had marched through the desert of Edom. Their water supply was depleted and they were despairing because of fear. The battle seemed hopeless. Dryness was threatening their lives. So they called on Elisha.

The Lord spoke to Elisha and told him that the answer was for the army to dig ditches. The last thing a thirsty person wants to do is dig a ditch! Nevertheless, the command of the Lord was obeyed and ditches were dug. The next morning at the time of sacrifice, a heavy rainstorm in the distant mountains of Edom caused a flash flood to rush through the valley where the army was. The ditches caught the water and were filled up, and the soldiers and their animals drank and were rejuvenated.

As the sun was rising, its reddish beams reflected off of the water in the red clay ditches. To the distant Moabite army, the water appeared as pools of blood and they thought the allied armies had turned on each other. The Moabites rushed in for the plunder only to find themselves facing strong and focused Israelite soldiers ready to die for God's glory (see 2 Kings 3)!

Spiritual disciplines can be compared in several ways with the ditches that the Lord commanded the Israelites to dig:

- Disciplines (like digging) are demanding work. Human nature
  shies away from such work and is quick to look for other dis-

tracting activities, and once started, finds it easy to stop without getting much done. The effects of these disciplines are spiritual, but the greatest obstacles come from the flesh.

· Disciplines (like ditches) are not ends in themselves. There is no glory in saying "I dig really great ditches" (or "I fast twice a week" or "I pray two hours a day"). It is the *water*—not the ditch—that brings life.

· The presence of water is not determined by whether or not a ditch has been dug. Water flows when it decides to rain—ditches merely contain and channel when it comes. Our spiritual habits give God opportunity, but do not obligate God's presence or power.

· God's mission will often take us across spiritual deserts, and ministry is a spiritual battle that cannot be won except through supernatural intervention. If we are thirsty, weak or embattled, the best thing we can do is dig ditches. Seeking God through fasting, prayer, scripture meditation, solitude and secret acts of service opens us to a fresh flow of the Holy Spirit.

· Disciplines increase our capacity to contain and communicate God's Spirit, just as Elisha's ditches contained the rushing water so that it was drinkable and communicated its presence to the Moabites. The deeper the ditches are dug through spiritual habits, the greater the capacity of a pastor to be effective as a carrier of God's Spirit.

· The water in Elisha's ditches had the appearance of blood, which was, perhaps, a foreshadowing of the blood of Christ as our source of victory. While the Moabites saw that "blood" as a sign of failure, the Lord used it for their defeat. Likewise, when spiritual disciplines are practiced well, they always lead to the power of the cross. When the enemy "sees red" in the life of a pastor, the battle will soon be over.

Making a Room

In his defining book *Celebration of Discipline*, Richard Foster describes three categories of discipline: *inward* (meditation, prayer, fasting and study), *outward* (simplicity, solitude, submission and service) and *corporate* (confession, worship, guidance and celebration).

Dallas Willard organizes the disciplines differently. In *The Spirit of the Disciplines*, he articulates two groupings: *abstinence* (solitude, silence, fasting, frugality, chastity, secrecy and sacrifice) and *engagement* (study, worship, celebration, service, prayer, fellowship, confession and submission).

However they are categorized, these habits of spiritual formation are paramount because they address the inner character of the pastor. They give access to the Holy Spirit to shape the soul, the mind, the heart and the will. They strip the pastor of title, position and popularity to address the essence of their identity and get below the surface to the roots of the issues in their lives.

Unfortunately, spiritual disciplines are often abused by pastors who turn them into a personal scorecard for their present level of spirituality. Ask a pastor who is deceived in this way, "How are you doing spiritually?" and the answer will be a batting average of his or her spiritual disciplines. The pastor describes the ditch and not the water.

Spiritual disciplines are not about routines (the ditch) but about relationship. If the spiritual habits of a pastor are only relieving his conscience, they are of little value and may even be counterproductive. The point of the disciplines is not task completion but relationship building.

There was a couple in Shunem who invited Elisha to dine with them. The encounter was so uplifting that Elisha started dropping in for dinner every time he passed through. One day the wife said to her husband, "Let's build an addition on the house so that Elisha can stay with us when he comes to town." They built the extra bedroom, furnished it and added amenities. Now, thanks to his new room, Elisha stayed for a few days every time he visited (see 2 Kings 4:8).

For the Shunem couple, the room wasn't the point—the point was building and strengthening a relationship with the prophet. The room didn't obligate Elisha to come to Shunem, but when he did, he stayed in the room that had been prepared for him.

Spiritual disciplines are the construction materials used to build a room for the Spirit to visit us. Some pastors want a deeper relationship with Christ, but they don't understand the need or won't pay the price to "build Him a room." The room is the outward action of spiritual disciplines that encourage the reality of spiritual relationship and personal transformation.

Ministry is about serving others. The occupational hazard is that attention to others can actually be about bringing attention to self and can compete with attention to Christ. Perhaps this is what Jesus saw when He made His visit to Martha and Mary's house. Martha's busyness appeared productive and commendable to the outward observer and Mary's focus on Jesus could be construed as lazy. Jesus, however, pronounced His opinion: "Martha, Martha," the Lord answered, "you are worried and upset about many things, but only one thing is needed. Mary has chosen what is better, and it will not be taken away from her" (Luke 10:41-42). Mary's choice was the necessary and the best response to Jesus, while Martha's produced worry, turbulence and fragmentation.

Spiritual disciplines are a form of choosing what Mary chose. By sitting at the feet of Jesus, Mary opened her life to the presence and teaching of the Master. By placing activity secondary to listening,

Mary commended an order of priorities for pastors. Spiritual habits seat us at the feet of Jesus so that His Spirit may address our lives before we arise to serve Him. There are six key ways that spiritual disciplines help us make room for the Holy Spirit:

1. Spiritual Disciplines Anchor Identity

Your pastoral self-image is under a constant barrage of positive and negative influences. The public nature of the role exposes you to the applause or critique of people on a weekly basis. The growth or lack of growth of the church, the financial blessings or shortages, the compliments or complaints of the board, the comparisons to other preachers, all join forces to blow your self-image onto the rocks of pride or inferiority. Spiritual disciplines are a means to anchor your identity to the truth of God's opinion. As you pray, meditate, fast, listen in silence, seek solitude, confess and submit to others, your soul is held fast and delivered from the destructive voices around you. The disciplines allow your identity to be shaped by the indwelling Spirit instead of surrounding voices.

The temptations of Jesus are the precursors to the temptations of our ministry. Jesus faced the seduction to use position to serve self instead of mission. He was tempted to put God on the spot to bless a display of personal glory. Satan tried to trick Jesus into submitting to false gods so that He could get to places of power more quickly and comfortably (see Matt. 4:1-11). These are the same battles that pastors wage. We are tempted to use our titles to stroke our egos, to leap into self-initiated plans while demanding God's blessing on the programs we've planned, and to look for the latest method to worship so that our churches grow faster.

In each of these temptations, Satan was attacking the identity of Jesus. "If you are the Son of God," Satan taunted Him, and threw down the gauntlet. However, Jesus stood solid in the knowledge of who He was and what God's Word said. How did Jesus do it? How can we?

First, at His baptism, which directly preceded the temptations, Jesus demonstrated the spiritual discipline of *submission* by submitting Himself both to John and to His Father. In that context, the Father spoke: "This is my Son, whom I love; with him I am well pleased" (Matt. 3:17). Hearing this affirmation of His identity from the Father centered and fortified Jesus against the voice of the enemy that was soon to come.

One of the most important purposes of the spiritual disciplines is to quiet our spirits enough to hear the voice of God speaking affirmation to us. To hear that we are sons or daughters, that we are loved for who we are and that we are already pleasing to God is liberation in its deepest form. Without His affirmation, we live in the insecurity of people's fickleness or the applause of our own egos, and we open ourselves to deceit.

Second, Jesus went into a time of *solitude, fasting* and *prayer* in the desert. These spiritual disciplines strengthened Jesus for the epic battle that He fought against Satan. Armed with a solid identity and an arsenal of spiritual disciplines, Jesus overcame the tempting voice of the deceiver—and so can you.

2. Spiritual Disciplines Center Activity

Ministry can quickly become disjointed. The distractions become so vivid and varied that centeredness is replaced by compartmentalization, and rather than moving through tasks with a singular focus on Christ, each task becomes the focus. We sometimes remember to "add a little Christ" to our activities, but He is no longer the center, and energy for ministry is drawn from shallow places of duty or demand. Soon the whirr of busyness and the whining voices of others are all we hear—the noise of ministry has drowned the voice of the Spirit. We operate on the peripheries of careerism instead of from a deep, unifying, centered place of connection with Christ. Spiritual disciplines can re-center our activity in Christ.

Jesus lived and ministered from this place of centeredness. He clearly stated, "the Son can do nothing on his own, he can only do whatever he sees his Father doing" (John 5:19). For Jesus, every ministry activity flowed out of union with the Father. He was not running around simply trying to do good works. He was not running ahead and asking God to catch up and bless His work.

If the wires on the back of my stereo get loose, the sound gets fuzzy. The wires have to be rewrapped tightly so that the clarity and fullness of the music can emerge. In the same way, spiritual disciplines wrap us tightly around Christ. Habits of spiritual formation provide a tight connection to drive our daily ministry so that we can move out in boldness and urgency instead of flailing, task-driven busyness. Our mission is clarified and our to-do list is unified. Our ears are tuned in. We lift up breath-prayers throughout the day to refocus us as the pressures of the day begin to blur our vision of Christ.

Christ must be the center of our pastorates. Ministry is from Him, through Him and to Him. Consequently, Christ must, in a very real manner, permeate all that is done for Him. It is only by saturating our souls in Christ through spiritual disciplines that we can live and minister from a well-formed center.

3. Spiritual Disciplines Refill Passion

Passion leaks. When I was in high school, I had a 1957 Ford flatbed truck that I used in my hay hauling business. I could stack 105 bales of hay on that truck. It had tons of power but two problems: a broken gas gauge and a leak in the gas tank. I'd be driving along, going strong, and suddenly that old truck would die. The holes had to be fixed and the tank refueled to be effective.

Our ministry tanks are often like my truck. Our spiritual energy gauges are broken—we don't know how to evaluate how spiritually full or empty we are, or we simply ignore the gauge, thinking we can drive forever. Rocks of criticism or disappointment hit our tank and cause pinhole leaks. They are so small that we think they're insignificant, but we desperately need repair and refilling if we plan to go the distance. Here is where spiritual disciplines become critical.

Spiritual disciplines allow the Spirit access to the places in our hearts that have been damaged because of the barbs of ministry. Often it's when I'm reading and meditating on the Word while at the same time writing in my journal that a revelation of my heart's condition happens. I see how I was injured by some passing critique and I'm able to confess my oversensitivity and receive healing affirmation from the Spirit. A callous that had grown in that place is removed. Tenderness is restored.

Last year, someone critiqued me in a way that was unfair and inaccurate. I was justifiably offended and was plotting how I would make them painfully aware of their mistake. However, as I was fasting, the Spirit said, "As you have given up food, give up your right to handle this. I will only handle it if you refuse to." I obeyed and watched God repair my heart and deal with the person without my help. Vengeance is an ugly attitude that can subtly creep into a pastor's heart. It tempts him to use his pulpit or his leadership to covertly even the score. It produces energy of emotion but drains spiritual energy. Often, a spiritual discipline involving self-denial (such as fasting or silence) can allow the Spirit access to the places in the heart where vengeance is planted so that He can uproot it and heal the wound.

Effective pastors understand that passion is essential to ministering well. They are honest about the drainage that real life causes to passion and they know which of the spiritual habits refills their zeal. The practice of these disciplines is mandatory for pastors—without them, they run out of gas. Our wounds cannot be ignored without causing leakage to our passion. Hurts are healed and holes repaired by surrender to the Spirit, and it is the disciplines that invite the Spirit to visit us and administer healing.

Once, the Lord gave me a mental picture of my heart. It was a vast desert. I saw a single garden hose being turned on and water beginning to wet the dry soil, but the difference it made to the parched earth was imperceptible. As more and more hoses were added, however, the soil began to grow lush green plants.

Likewise, the more spiritual disciplines that are "turned on" the greater the opportunity for your heart and ministry to flourish. There is power that results from the spiritual disciplines—not from the practices themselves, but from the Spirit pouring through them to rejuvenate and reenergize our lives.

4. Spiritual Disciplines Sensitize the Spirit

Spiritual disciplines grow spiritual discernment. The pastor who is employing the disciplines will find her ability to sense the presence of good and evil more finely honed, much like the metal detectors at the airport: The finer-tuned they are, the better they can prevent dangerous items from getting onto the aircraft. Pastors who operate without this discernment soon find their churches filled with explosive philosophies, un-Christlike attitudes and destructive spiritual strongholds.

The practice of the disciplines can quicken the heart, mind, eyes and ears of a pastor so that she can see these weapons and prevent them from being used to hurt her church. The writer of Hebrews talks about people with this kind of sensitivity: "Who by constant use have trained themselves to distinguish good from evil" (Heb. 5:14). Studying, memorizing, meditating, reading and praying the Word of God trains us this way. Solitude, silence, confession, simplicity, worship and fasting sharpen our spirits.

A few years ago, I was inspired by Bill Bright to go on a 40-day fast. By the end of that fast, my nose was so sensitive that I could smell a McDonald's French fry from 40 yards away! But I also remember how sensitized I was to the spiritual realm, to what pleased or displeased

God, and to the spiritual forces that were present. My eyes were opened to a few issues that had previously seemed harmless, but which held underlying seeds of destruction.

Part of the role of pastor is to care for and protect people from hurtful and damaging attitudes and patterns. These can rob your church of health through an insidious invasion and no one may realize it. You are effective when your discernment is honed through disciplined formation.

5. Spiritual Disciplines Build Christlikeness

The ultimate goal of spiritual disciplines is to train our hearts to be more and more conformed to the image of Christ. The goal of every truly effective pastor is to live like Christ in daily life, and his or her spiritual disciplines are oriented toward explicit obedience to Christ in all things.

Pastors are not zapped into Christlikeness. It's not attained by some high-octane spiritual experience that happens at the right conference. Neither do pastors work themselves into Christlikeness. The efforts of the flesh will always meet with failure, even when directed toward noble goals. Cooperation with the Spirit is the only means by which progress is made.

It's similar to scaffolding in construction. If you are building a tall wall, you need to erect scaffolding. The scaffolding does not build the wall; it allows the builders to have access to the wall so that they can do the building. Spiritual disciplines provide a place for the Master Builder to stand while He shapes our lives into Christlikeness. By grace we provide the scaffolding and by grace the Spirit does His work.

When Paul told Timothy, "Train yourself to be godly" (1 Tim. 4:7), he was not suggesting that the young pastor could attain Christlikeness by trying really hard. The training that Paul challenged was to imitate the spiritual activities that Jesus had modeled so that the life of Christ might be formed in Timothy. The work of training invites the work of the Spirit.

As Dallas Willard says, "Grace is opposed to earning but it is not opposed to effort."[1] We give our effort to give the Spirit access to our hearts.

The metaphor that Paul used in 1 Timothy is a reference to an athlete's preparation for the Greek games. Competitors stripped down and practiced naked in the gymnasium. The kind of training that pastors need is one in which their self-protection, denial, pride and any other "fig leaf" they might hide behind is stripped away, baring the heart before God and bringing them to greater vulnerability and dependence on the Spirit.

Effective pastors are not trying to live the life of Jesus. They are trying to live their own life like Jesus would if He were in their place. Pastors must live without a savior complex and, at the same time, live with a Christlikeness that serves as a model for the congregation. Pastors who make the imitation of Christ their highest aspiration will find that spiritual disciplines are a primary means of progressing toward that goal. Without them, a pastor will have a difficult time saying, "Imitate me as I imitate Christ" (see 1 Cor. 11:1).

6. Spiritual Disciplines Empower Teaching

In order for the teaching of a pastor to be fresh and powerful, it cannot be copied off the Internet or out of a book. It cannot even only be insights that have been dug out of careful study of Scripture. There is more to conveying the truth of the Word.

Jesus described the nature of His truth in John 6:63: "The Spirit gives life; the flesh counts for nothing. The words I have spoken to you are spirit and they are life." The words of Jesus are spiritual words that give life when they are understood by the help of the Holy Spirit. The pastor's task, then, is not simply to understand the meaning of the words but *to encounter the spirit of the words*. The spiritual disciplines are a means for the Holy Spirit to teach both the truth and the power of the words.

The pastor who practices the disciplines begins to fill her life with spiritual treasures. When she speaks, she does not do so merely from an intellectual or philosophical understanding, passing on principles she has studied. She is not speaking from her head, but from her heart. Jesus says in Luke 6:45, "The good man brings good things out of the good stored up in his heart . . . For out of the overflow of his heart his mouth speaks." Spiritual disciplines are a means for you to store up good things in your heart and then to speak from that overflow.

*   *   *

Without regular habits of spiritual formation, your inner life will become anemic and contrived. Ministry will flow from a shallow performance orientation. It may appear effective to those watching, but the internal dryness cannot continue without resulting damage to the congregation. Digging deep ditches of spiritual disciplines catches the flow of God's Spirit, bringing the victory pastors long for in their own lives and health and abundant life among their people.

Note

1. Dallas Willard, "Live Life to the Full," *Christian Herald* (UK), April 14, 2001. http://www.dwillard.org/articles/artview.asp?artID=5 (accessed January 2007).

Jeremiah 10:21 says, "The shepherds are senseless and do not inquire of the Lord; so they do not prosper and all their flock is scattered." The shepherds fail because they act without wisdom and neglect God in prayer.

Effective pastors love pursuing wisdom in their leadership. They are quick to ask God for insight into their ministries. They prioritize prayer as a means through which God guides their church.

"Then I will give you shepherds after my own heart, who will lead you with knowledge and understanding" (3:15). These effective shepherds know and share God's compassionate heart for people. They lead with knowledge of God's truth that can be lived in practical ministry. According to Jeremiah, these shepherds combine heart and head, care and leadership.

PERSONAL INTEGRITY:

Values and consistently manifests personal integrity

Gino was my neighbor. He lived alone most of the time. He was a tall, well built, middle-aged man who wore tinted glasses and worked as a carpenter in the active housing boom. He had a faithful friend in the aging German shepherd that he called "Junior," and on occasion, when he forgot or couldn't pay his utility bill, he would ask to hook his hose to our water faucet so that he could have water. We were neighbors for nine years.

Over those years, our family saw various women stay with Gino for long and short periods of time. One moved in and a few months (or weeks) later, she moved out . . . followed shortly by another. Usually the move-outs were preceded by an increased frequency of loud arguments, laced with words never before heard by our young children, drifting over the wall and into our family room door.

We had never smelled pot before living next door to Gino, but a strange aroma would not infrequently waft through the windows on the warm summer evening breeze. And Gino always spoke his mind. Our occasional conversations revealed that trait quickly, especially after he found out I was a "man of the cloth."

Once I was laying brick just outside the front door of our house to make a patio-like front entrance and was thwarted by a three-inch iron pipe sticking up from the ground. It needed to be cut shorter so that I could lay the brick over it, so I grabbed my hacksaw and began cutting.

After 15 minutes of effort, my back ached, my breath was short and sweat was pouring off my forehead in the summer heat—and a minor scratch on the pipe was the only result of my hard work. I fell back against the house, exhausted and frustrated.

I noticed Gino across the front lawn, leaning against the wall of his garage, legs crossed, smoking a cigarette and watching me. It suddenly occurred to me that he knew all about construction and houses and pipes and might have a tool that would help, so I called out and asked.

Gino disappeared into his garage for a few seconds and came out with a handheld, battery-operated reciprocating saw. He sauntered over with his cigarette dangling from his lips, squatted down, revved up the saw and in five seconds cut the pipe down to size. I stood there stunned. Finally I choked out, "You mean you were watching me struggle with that pipe this whole time and knew you could cut it off in a heartbeat?"

His response took me off guard. "Well, I was wondering how long your pride would keep you from asking for help!"

Gino never made any pretense of being something he was not. What you saw or heard was what you got, and his life was consistent with his words. He was authentic in his relationship with me—sometimes hurtful, but at least genuine.

I, on the other hand, felt a need not to appear weak or incapable in front of Gino, and in the process spent a lot of sweat trying to preserve my image. That encounter on my front lawn made me think of integrity in a new way. I realized that many Christians (especially pastors) feel the need to portray an image that may not be consistent with who we really are.

Often in our contemporary discussions of integrity, we attach virtuous qualities to it as a way of understanding the concept—but when we do so, we muddy the waters instead of gaining clarity. When I ask people to tell me what integrity is, the response is often that "integrity" is synonymous with words like:

Goodness	Godliness
Righteousness	Holiness
Morality	Justice
Truthfulness	Humility
Honor	Virtue

These are great words, but what happens when they are redefined by the culture around us? Does integrity shift right along with them? Or is there another dimension to integrity that can help us as we seek to develop this characteristic in our lives and ministries?

Integrity: A Definition

Occasionally when I ask someone to define integrity for me, they will describe a sound and strong relationship between the parts of a whole, such as the "foundational integrity" of a building or the "structural integrity" of a car body. A building's foundation has integrity if its parts work together and are integrated such that it can support the weight and pressure of the elements and daily use, and a car body has integrity if its parts fit together rightly to withstand extensive travel or even a crash.

Integrity is the continuity between two or more parts, integrated to form an undivided whole. With that understanding, then, someone possesses integrity if there is consistency between who he or she is and what he or she does. Does he purport to be someone he is not? Does he represent himself as someone he is not? Do his actions cast doubt on the claims he makes about himself? If so, then he cannot, by definition, have integrity. (I wonder if Gino had more integrity than many Christians who lay claim to Christ but reflect Him poorly!) Effective pastors prioritize the internal and private realms of obedience more than the external, public arena of appearance, and this integrity—the continuity between the internal and external—creates credibility.

There is a helpful analogy found in the book *The Integrity Factor*[1] that captures the spirit of integrity: The bottom of an iceberg is beneath the waterline where no one can see, while the top is above the waterline, visible to anyone around. The bottom comprises 90 percent of the whole iceberg, while the top is only 10 percent.

Imagine that the iceberg represents your life. The bottom of the iceberg is your identity (who you are, your character, your inner being) and the top of the iceberg is your activity (what you do, your performance, your tasks for work, home or school). You cannot separate who you are from what you do any more than you can separate the bottom of the iceberg from the top. They are one.

Your identity is the basis for your activity—it is out of your character that you behave. Activities are flavored, shaped and guided by identity. Just as the bottom of the iceberg gives stability, buoyancy and definition to the top of the iceberg, so also, who you are is reflected in what you do.

The bottom of the iceberg deals with the question "Who am I?" The top of the iceberg deals with "What am I here to do?" The bottom deals with the *fruit* of the Spirit and the top deals with the *gifts* of the Spirit. You cannot separate one from the other: Gifts flow out of a character that is well formed and shaped by the character of Christ, and spiritual fruit is bestowed by God's grace to find expression in the ministry activities to which you are called.

You're Not What You Do

One of the greatest traps of ministry is answering bottom-of-the-iceberg questions with top-of-the-iceberg answers. Here's how that works:

Someone asks, "Who are you?"

"I'm a teacher."

"I'm an engineer."

"I'm a pastor."

"I'm a painter."

Well, no—not really. Those are things that you *do*, but they should not define your identity. Admittedly, we engage in that kind of conversation almost every day as a social nicety that will probably never change. But I hope that from this point on, every time someone asks you who you are, you will experience a small niggle in the back of your mind, reminding you that your identity is not defined by what you do.

When you define who you are based on what you do, you become a slave to your own performance. When that performance is poor, you might conclude that you are a bad person and look for affirmation in other places, places you should not go—misbehavior, illicit relationships, problem habits. A pastor in that condition is looking for personal affirmation of who he is because the measure of his identity (what he does) has been found wanting. It happens to pastors often, and it's perhaps the greatest cause of burnout and moral failure in ministry.

Conversely, if your performance is stellar and more successful than you expected, you might conclude that you are good—*really good*. So good, in fact, that you can live above the rules that were meant for everyone else. If performance is the basis of identity, it is easy for a high-performing pastor to begin experimenting beyond the limits of propriety, assuming that she is better than others and that she is the exception. That kind of entitlement attitude can quickly undermine the effectiveness of ministry.

Types of Integrity

Integrity, as we have described above, is continuity between the bottom and the top of the iceberg. A lack of integrity exists when who we are and what we do are not consistent with one another. This understanding of integrity, however, introduces an interesting idea that we do not often consider.

Let's assume that X = Good and Y = Bad. In the following "iceberg" models, notice how integrity can be either Good or Bad, because it is a function of *consistency* rather than *moral or ethical value*. Integrity happens when the top of the iceberg—the part above the water line—and the bottom match up.

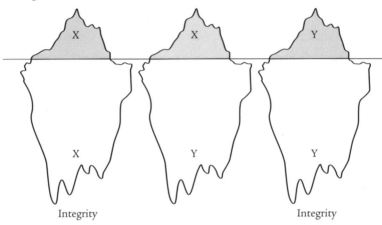

Even though he may be "Bad," the third person has integrity because there is consistency between who he is and what he does, much like my neighbor Gino. Gino never claimed to be a good person. He didn't say he was holy, good, right or pure and then live his life in the opposite direction. He lived who he was and I appreciated his honesty. (I think God did, too.) At least Gino was cold to the things of Christ. He wasn't lukewarm, misrepresenting himself in actions devised to make him look better than he really was. Jesus says that He will spit the lukewarm person out of His mouth (see Rev. 3:16).

Thankfully, as time went on, Gino became more and more responsive to the love of God for him—but he only listened because he saw that I did not live a lie, either. Consistency between who you are and what you do may be the most important factor in a pastor's ministry. Others notice.

Let's consider three types of integrity in which leaders always engage.

1. Behavioral Integrity
This is the most basic level of integrity, and we have already begun to examine it. Simply put, behavioral integrity is continuity between who

you are and what you do. You don't put on a façade or try to portray an image of something or someone that you're not.

The confidence of the people in your church will be shaken if they sense a lack of behavioral integrity through odd behavior or mixed signals. This will undermine your effectiveness because they assume you have something to hide or an ulterior motive. On the other hand, when you guard your heart and pursue integrity, your people will grow in their respect and support as they discern a life that is consistent. This is one of the most important tributes given to pastors: "She is authentic to who she is."

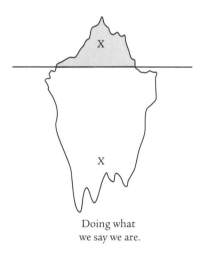

Doing what
we say we are.

Behavioral integrity is that condition wherein you freely and naturally reflect your identity in your behavior. The top of the iceberg reflects the bottom.

2. Performance Integrity

Though most everyone is aware of performance integrity to a certain extent, it is particularly important for leaders—especially Christian leaders. Performance integrity is the relationship between what you do and the people who are affected by your actions. As a leader, you must be cognizant of the impact you have and do what you say you will do—follow-through, being true to your word. Do not mislead or manipulate, but deal with people in a manner that affirms them and builds their dignity. (Of course, if performance integrity is the primary motivator for you, it can become an unhealthy focus on people pleasing.)

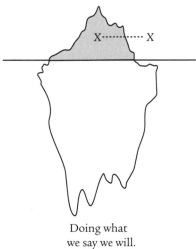

X⋯⋯⋯X

Doing what
we say we will.

Remember that when you speak or make a decision, you represent the office of pastor and, in a mysterious way, carry the trust of every pastor with you. Carry this responsibility with appropriate seriousness, because if you fail to practice performance integrity, *every* pastor suffers as the trust, confidence and respect of your people is diminished and they view all pastors with doubt and suspicion.

3. Internal Integrity

This is perhaps the most difficult type to describe because it is integrity of the interior life. The pursuit of spiritual formation is largely an effort to bring consistency to the inner dimensions of your life, which is vital to a healthy and vibrant life and call. There is always a temptation to compartmentalize your internal life so that your spiritual life is kept separate from your psychological makeup, personality, talents and will.

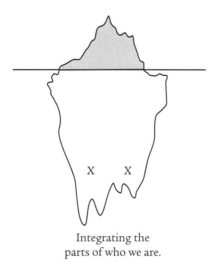

Integrating the
parts of who we are.

A life that is internally compartmentalized always winds up manifesting that fragmentation in behaviors that are likewise disconnected and segmented—remember that who we are *always* finds expression in what we do. If you do not allow the spiritual dimension of your inner life to affect your emotions, your personality and even your physical body, you will behave in a spiritual way during spiritual activities, and then rage at home with your spouse and children, or talk of the need for disciplined spiritual practices and then habitually overeat.

We have been created as integrated beings, and cultivating internal integration leads to abundance and wholeness. *Leadership Journal's* editor-at-large, Gordon MacDonald, wrote this about a pastor of integrity: "This is a person who takes seriously the insights and principles of Scripture and has sought *to organize all of life around them.* What you see in public is what you might see in private. There is no discontinuity in the whole of this person's life."[2]

Ways to Build Identity and Integrity

You may be asking, "Okay, so how can I build my identity so that it maintains a strong influence on my actions?" In other words, how do you build the bottom of your iceberg? Without intentional effort to build your identity in Christ, your life will default to its natural self-defensive inclinations, protecting an external image that is increasingly out of synch with your identity. There are three key ways to keep your character sound and strong.

1. Spiritual Disciplines

Disciplines of the spiritual life are activities (top of the iceberg) that affect identity (bottom of the iceberg). It may seem counterintuitive that we must "do" something to deepen our "being," but that is the mysterious way God has created us. In doing certain behaviors habitually, we are shaped inwardly.

I recently talked with a man who, because of an extramarital affair, was on the verge of a broken marriage five years ago. He recalled that he had asked me at that time, "How do I change my nature?"

My answer to him was, "Layer changed daily behaviors one upon the other, and your nature will begin to change, too." Today that man's character *is* changed—his nature is being reformed in a new and healthy way. While it may seem odd that our identity can be deepened through actions, that's the way it works—but it requires discipline and perseverance.

2. Proximity of Others

Imagine that you are in a boat on the north Atlantic and you see an iceberg from a great distance. The only part you can see is the top. At such a distance, the angle of your sight requires you to look through too much water to see the bottom.

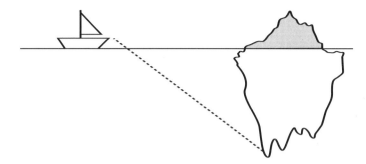

However, if you draw near the iceberg, you discover that you can look straight down through the clear water to see the bottom of the iceberg.

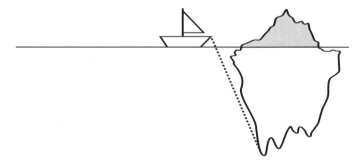

In a similar way, when wise, godly people are kept at a distance from you, they can't see the bottom of your identity. They can't encourage you about the continuity or confront you about the discontinuity between who you are and what you are doing. It is important to invite a few trustworthy others to sail right up next to you to look down and see who you are. In close proximity, they can affirm you or hold you accountable for a lack of integrity that is not visible at a distance.

Letting a few others come that close may be frightening, because it gives them access to the deep recesses of who you are. Vulnerability is an act of the will—not simply transparency, but vulnerability. *Transparency* shows another person parts of yourself while you retain control. You show him or her what you want him or her to know about you and that person cannot hurt you. *Vulnerability*, on the other hand, opens you to the scrutiny of another person to the point at which he or she can hurt you with what he or she knows and reject you if he or she chooses.

Integrity is strengthened by choosing to be vulnerable with a small number of trusted people. It is not a sign of weakness—quite the contrary. Consider the greatest model of vulnerability: God. Out of a desire to know us, God chose to be vulnerable to us, to be open to us—even to the point of being rejected by us. The cross represents the supreme rejection that was the consequence of God's vulnerability. Following God's example is not weakness. It builds strength when it springs from a deep desire to know God, ourselves and others.

3. The Spirit's Witness

At a mysterious level that transcends our ability to describe, the Holy Spirit witnesses that we are rooted in Christ, that we are truly children of God. While words cannot explain the means by which this witness strengthens the bottom of our iceberg, the interface with the Spirit is very real and assures us that God's image is being molded in us.

This inner witness deals in the realm of motive and intention. It is one thing to replicate the behavior of Jesus to whatever degree we are able: We are confronted with a tough situation and ask, "What would Jesus do?" But it is a deeper work of God in us that allows the *motives* of Christ to become our motives. This is the work of becoming Christlike: The heart of God is manifested through Christ and through those who are becoming like Him.

When you are building the bottom of your iceberg, strengthening the integrity of your life by bringing continuity between who you are and what you do, reflect on the inner witness of the Holy Spirit to examine your motives and your intentions. Do they reflect the motives of Christ? Are they consistent with the heart of God's love? Is there deep assurance that who you are is pleasing to the Lord? This regular practice of reflection and contemplation is an indispensable part of strengthening your integrity because it helps to ensure proper motives when projecting a pastoral image.

* * *

Integrity, perhaps more than any other trait, is always at stake in pastoral ministry. The temptations of power, position, image, importance, ego building—to say nothing of the more visceral drives like money, sex and addictions—are always knocking at the pastor's heart, but there is no greater detriment to effectiveness than a lack of personal integrity. When there is a lack of continuity between who a pastor is and what a pastor does, credibility, influence and trust are quickly lost and are difficult (if not impossible) to regain.

Years ago as I neared the end of seminary, I watched as the seminary seniors tried to determine where they would go to fulfill their call. Each year, denominational leaders descended on the campus to interview promising young candidates, and I witnessed these "meat market" days (as they came to be known) firsthand.

As friends and classmates went to interviews with high hopes, naturally I asked how the meetings went. My queries were mostly met with the appropriate response that prayer and ongoing dialogue would determine what was best for the church and for the candidate. But a few troubled me.

In a couple of cases, the candidate replied, "Oh, fine . . . but I'm holding out for a bigger salary" or "I'm waiting for one with a parsonage" or "I want something in Florida or Southern California." At the time it was a bit funny, but I had to wonder: Was pastoring a calling or a job? What was the true motive for these future leaders? Was it to share the love of God for people, or was it to establish comfortable, secure careers and incomes for themselves?

Most of those candidates are no longer in ministry. The lack of consistency between who they were in their character and motives, and what they did in their words, actions and decisions caused a disintegration that led to ineffective pastoral leadership.

To believe that effectiveness can exist where integrity does not is misguided. This fact does not presume that effective pastors are all perfect and never fail at the point of integrity. But even in the failure, integrity is the essential ingredient to restore health and wholeness that reflect the character of God, and to usher in renewed effectiveness to follow the call of God.

Notes
1. Kevin W. Mannoia, *The Integrity Factor: A Journey in Leadership Formation* (Vancouver, B.C.: Regent Press, 2006), n.p.
2. Gordon MacDonald, written comments on the *15 Characteristics of Effective Pastors*.

MARTIN LUTHER (1483-1546) AND
JOHN CALVIN (1509-1564)

Martin Luther stressed the functions of pastors including the ministry of the Word, baptizing, administration of the sacred bread and wine, binding and loosing sins, and sacrifice. He put great emphasis on pastoral care, which always related directly to the ministry of the Word.

John Calvin saw effectiveness as successfully carrying out the roles of preaching, governing and pastoring. His concern was the profit and education of the hearer. To this responsibility, he added the important issues of administration of the sacraments and visitation of the sick.

LOVE FOR THE CHURCH:

Demonstrates a love and zeal for the Church of Jesus Christ through his or her actions

"Let's go to church today!" Off the family goes in the car, down the street, around a few corners or, in some cases, a 30-minute ride on the freeway. They clamber out of the car, scattering in different directions to different rooms where each of them participates in a different activity. At the appointed hour, everybody meets at the same pew to sit through the preliminaries, after which the kids take off to yet another location for a special program to keep them interested while the adults stay for the sermon.

After mingling and catching up with friends, and the starts and stops through the foyer and parking lot, everybody piles in the car for a quick drive to Carl's Jr., Taco Bueno or (if they're lucky) the Grand Buffet Palace. The rush begins to wind down on arrival at home as people drift off to homework, naps or football. Everybody's happy—they went to church! What an experience—you gotta love it!

George Barna, the trend analyst and strategic leader, has been criticized as being anti-Church. He suggests that we've eviscerated the Church by redefining it as a cultural experience and that we've missed the point. He believes that the Church is not a program, with the optional premium package that includes lunch and a football game as a free bonus.[1]

Everyone is entitled to his or her own opinion, but I think Barna is one of the most optimistic people I know. Who in the world invests his life in a dying proposition? If the Church were truly a lost cause, I don't think he would pour himself into understanding it and raising the alarm. What we've created in the institutional church may not be attractive or effective, but the Church about which George Barna is hopeful—the Bride and Body of Christ—is vibrant and real.

Effective pastors are positive and passionate about the nature and mission of the local and global Church, and their love manifests itself in selfless acts of courageous leadership that guide the Church into maturity and outreach. They possess a deep love for the kingdom of God in the world, reflected in the Body of Christ. They are neither deluded by false images that claim to be the Church, nor misguided by institutional activities that distract from the authentic Church. They may be disillusioned by how we have reframed and redefined "church" (like Barna), but they remain hopeful and confident that God, in His mercy, can continue to use His Bride to accomplish His work in the world. They see beyond the trappings and frills to the real fiber of the Church and have tapped into the lifeblood of God's work. After all, the Church is God's means to establish His kingdom on Earth as it is in heaven! That vision is what effective pastors fall in love with.

The love relationship starts with a deepening understanding of what the Church really is. Is the Church a gift of God that Christ-followers receive and discover? Is the Church present wherever "two or three are gathered"? Does it come from the presence of the saints? Do people enter into the organic Body by identifying with Christ? You must engage, reflect, pray and study to be at peace with these questions. Wherever you wind up in your ecclesiology, whatever direction you tilt in your understanding of the Church, one thing is clear: It is the Body of Christ through which the Holy Spirit works for God's purposes in the world.

Effective pastors cultivate a love for both the universal Church and the local church. (Where we have used Church with a capital C, we are referring to the universal Church, the living Body of Christ, while the small c church refers to the institutional or local church.)

The Universal Church

One of the biggest questions facing leaders today is, What is the nature and mission of the Church? Church councils down through the ages have struggled with it. Ecumenical meetings and studies have been fueled by it. Some people conclude that it is evidence of a divided Church. Some even presume to say that if we have to ask, we are not worthy to be called Christians.

Every time I have seen people gathered to honestly address the question, however, I have discovered deep wells of love and zeal for the Church. In the debates, heated though they may be, I see passion to understand the mysterious work of God. I see yearning for God to shape the Body of Christ as a reflection of the Kingdom. In the relationships that result from people struggling with the question, I see unity and solidarity that can only be attributed to the work of God, even if differences remain. When I see people engage the question at a global, national or local level, I see steps taken toward deeper love and greater zeal for the Church.

When *you* engage the question of the Church's nature and mission, mining the wisdom of the Spirit and wrestling with others who are just as passionate, you too will find your love and zeal for the Church beginning to grow. You may never answer it, but that's not the point. The desire that drives the question and the exploration that follows will have their intended effect on your deepening love for the Church.

Notice that Characteristic 5 has two very important aspects: *love* and *zeal*. Love has to do with the *nature* of the Church while zeal is related to the *mission* of the Church.

Love is a total commitment of the will in response to deep knowledge of something or someone. True love cannot exist where there is ignorance about the person's nature, his identity or his character. Love emanates from and responds to the nature of the beloved. Your leadership should demonstrate a love for the Church—the Body of Christ—that flows from knowing the nature of the Church.

Zeal is love finding its expression in action. Zeal flows from the deeper well of love but is only evident when it is engaged in action. Your leadership must demonstrate active zeal for the Church as a product of your love for the Church. Your zeal must be informed and guided by what you know about the nature of the Church and its purposes in the world. In other words, zeal is active participation in the mission of the Church.

You may be asking, "How can I learn to love the Church?" Great question. The answer is, *Love doesn't just happen*. It's not a spontaneous emotion. You choose to love and you learn to love, and love for the Church starts by deepening your love for the Lord of the Church—the Head, Jesus Christ. (Funny how all the characteristics of effective pastors come back to that: pursuing knowledge of God, love for Jesus and intimacy with the Holy Spirit—it stands to reason, though, because the Church and your calling as a pastor all emanate from God's desire to share His love with all the world. You can't share it if you haven't experienced it yourself!)

The Local Church

The local church is Christian community at its best, as the people of God reflect the principles of the Kingdom: Love one another. Encourage one another. Bear one another's burdens. Rejoice with one another. Confess your sins to one another. Speak the truth in love to one another. These principles, when practiced, reflect Christ at work in community. That is church.

At times, pastors may need to work to preserve Christian community as the essence of their church, and doing so may require risky or painful decisions. It may mean putting themselves on the line to protect the local Body. When something you love is challenged, you're willing to take risks to defend it. That's the nature of love.

Maybe you find yourself shying away from these difficult decisions, operating out of expediency—making decisions that seem safe, but that gradually gnaw away at the Body of Christ. You find yourself ducking everyday challenges to the life of the church:

"Should we sue the volunteer who stole our equipment?"

"Do I tell the church millionaire that his money doesn't make him the boss?"

"Can I let the divisive spirit continue among us?"

It's easy to let these kinds of issues take their own course and hope that doing so will save you from criticism and personal hurt. But in the process, the church gets hurt, and Jesus longs to see His Bride preserved by and nurtured with the Kingdom principles that proceed from His Spirit.

I'm not saying that pastors should see every threat or obstacle as a cause to fight, but when the essence of Christian community is being compromised in your church, how do you respond? Are you cowardly? Do you let it happen and try to rationalize your negligence? If so, you probably don't really love the church. You may love the *idea* of the church. You may even love the place you hold in the church. But you have lost the passion that propels you zealously into action to defend what you love . . . and you are probably not very effective.

Because the church is both divine (indwelt with the Holy Spirit) and human (comprised of people), there is both a spiritual and an institutional element to its nature. The institutional element allows the spiritual nature to find form in a way people can understand—it is tangible. We can see it. We can understand it because it is an organization that we can relate to. The spiritual element, on the other hand, is what makes the church an organism, not merely an organization. It is the life of the church, sustained by the very presence of Christ.

An effective pastor recognizes and seeks to preserve this dynamic balance. The institutional side of the church is not discarded as unspiritual, nor does it become so important that it quenches the vitality that comes from the Spirit. Balance and a healthy respect for both are woven together out of love for what the church represents—the Spirit of Christ at work among people.

Because the church is indwelt with the presence of God, it is not merely an institution and is not to be manipulated by self-centered leaders to build their own empires. Pastors who profit from the church do so at their own peril and to the detriment of other leaders. In their profiteering, they besmirch and prostitute what is meant to be a vibrant manifestation of Christ, bringing the kingdom of God near. Effective pastors will be revolted by such perversions.

*   *   *

Do you remember when you first fell in love with your spouse? Or maybe your first boyfriend or girlfriend? You couldn't get enough information about that person. You wanted to spend time with him or her to learn everything about him or her. You asked questions, listened to what others said about that person, read his or her writing. You did everything you could to discover details about that person.

You want to learn to love the Church? Study and learn about its nature. Understanding the nature of the Church means that you explore all aspects of it. You study it, pursue it, ask about it, open yourself to it—*you know it*. As you get to know its nature, your love for the Church will grow, and as your love grows, your zeal for the Church's mission will thrive with passion and power.

Note

1. George Barna explores these ideas in his excellent book *Revolution* (Carol Stream, IL: Tyndale House Publishers, 2006).

BIBLICAL FOUNDATIONS:

EPHESIANS 4

Poimen is the Greek word translated "pastor" in the New Testament. The only time *poimen* is used in the New Testament to mean an office of the church is in Ephesians 4:11: "He gave . . . and some to be pastors and teachers." The use of "and some" to cover both "pastors and teachers" and the omission of the article before "teachers," strongly suggests that these offices were intended to be considered together as an expression of a single office. This infers that teaching is a significant function of the pastoral office.

The effective pastor assumes the responsibility to influence the worldviews and actions of her people. She heartily embraces her role as a teacher and uses all available means to impart the truth of God into lives. She understands that her life teaches more than her words.

SERVANT LEADER:

*Demonstrates a godly servant attitude
in personal and leadership roles*

She was an intelligent, bright-eyed graduate student who was full of life, potential and a desire to learn. Kara entered the classroom early and selected a seat in the center of the U-shaped tables, directly opposite where I would sit and stand to lead the class. She opened her laptop, laid her books on the table in front of her and bounced in her seat as she prepared herself for the first class of the term.

As I do with every student who comes in for the first night of class, I walked over, stuck out my hand and introduced myself: "Hi, glad you're here. What's your name?"

"Kara," she said, "and I am so glad to be in this class . . . I almost thought I wouldn't get in before it filled up."

"Oh?" I said, flattered that people were rushing to fill my class. "And why are you so excited about this particular class?"

"Well, because I've heard so much about servant leadership and I'm dying to learn more . . . 'cause I heard it really works!"

I knew at that moment that I had a task on my hands. Kara was probably one of hundreds of people who have taken that class for the same reason: They've heard that "servant leadership works" and they want to get an edge with the latest and best "technique" to increase their chances of being a good leader or effective boss. To them, servant leadership is just the latest system trend to developing leadership skills. If they don't learn it, they'll drop behind the cutting edge in "leadership technology."

In the last few years, the idea of servant leadership has become a fad, a novelty in leadership studies. As a recent addition to academia, "leadership studies" is looking for its own sets of models, styles, theories and best practices that will legitimize it as an academic discipline. Servant leadership, to many, is the latest and best model.

Robert Greenleaf, in his classic book *Servant Leadership,* provided a starting point for the rapidly expanding network of centers, books and events focused on the innovative premise of putting others first. Greenleaf defined servant leadership in terms of the relationship between a leader and those whom he or she leads: "The great leader is seen as servant first, and that simple fact is the key to his greatness."[1]

In the past few years, the idea has caught on in secular and sacred environments alike.[2] Christian leaders find familiarity in the basic ideas underlying the principles: Servant leadership is a model that best represents the oft-conflicting values of a humble and Christlike life, and a position requiring initiative, boldness and leadership.

The problem is not with the first articulation of servant leadership. Greenleaf's book and subsequent works that expand on the concept sound the clear call to solid, empowered leadership. The problem lies with the perception that servant leadership is a *style* of leadership, lined up alongside other styles from which the leader can choose.

Servanthood Is Not a Fad

There is a pattern that occurs when a new idea comes on the scene. The first generation to adopt and articulate the new idea embodies the principles internally but describes them with objective words and behaviors. Along come followers who hear the words and observe the behaviors and, in their enthusiasm, "preach the gospel" of the principles by emphasizing the words and behaviors. In the long-run, because they have not internalized the core principles, they end up redefining them as mere imitation of those words and behaviors.

In some respect, this is the cycle occurring with the idea of servant leadership. While it is nothing new—inasmuch as it comes from the heart of God and is best exemplified in the life of Jesus—it has found renewed interest in contemporary leadership studies with the help of business leaders and theoreticians. The fresh recognition of servant leadership is a wonderful discovery for many leaders in corporate and educational fields, and the rise of interest in servant leadership within Christian circles has led to its application in a variety of situations, ranging from positional leadership to marriage.[3] But with all of the excitement surrounding the "new" idea, pastors must not fall prey to the misconception that servant leadership is merely a set of words and behaviors.

Servant leadership is much more than a style of leadership. It is not in competition with "participatory leadership" or "contingency leadership" or "autocratic leadership" or "*laissez-faire* leadership" or any other style you wish to add to the list. When it is relegated to such a "style catalog," servant leadership gets lost in the sea of options and fails to serve pastors as an underlying foundation for effectiveness in ministry.

Servant leadership is at the core of effectiveness in pastoral leadership. Effective pastors approach every relationship with a mind-set of servanthood that asks, "How can I encourage you so that you feel valued and empowered to follow God's destiny for your life?" This humility of leadership is bold enough to direct people, but is always motivated by God's purposes—not personal gain.

Kara was so excited to learn the latest technology, to acquire the newest skill and apply it. But in our class, she did not learn how to *do* servant leadership—the discipline, the style, the method. What she learned was what it means to *be* a servant leader. When Kara finished the class a few months later, she wrote, "I never thought I would learn so much about myself and who I am. I get it."

Servant leadership is a *condition*, not a style. It is a condition of the leader in her identity. At the risk of confusing you, servant leaders can use various styles of leadership and be effective, because servanthood is not in competition with leadership styles—it is fundamental to them all, especially in a Kingdom context. You may have a personality, gifting and experiences that lend themselves to a particular style of leadership, and that's okay. That style will not be effective, however, until it is rooted in a servant-leader identity. The Church is not just another organization, and leading within it requires the alignment of its leaders to the nature of its Head. Servant leadership is putting on the servant-mind of Christ and allowing that nature to influence whatever style of leadership is most appropriate to your gifting.

Jesus: The Servant Leader

The fountainhead of servant leadership is Jesus Christ, and one of the best places to find the principle clearly at work is in the *kenosis* passage.[4] Jesus accepted the call of the Father to take human form. Doing so required two things: First, it required that He empty Himself of His rights as God. He did not hang on to those rights in a defensive manner, but loosened His grip on what was His in order to fulfill the call of the Father, reconciling people back to their Creator and restoring the wholeness God desired for them.

Second, His call required that He humble Himself. Emptying has to do with rights, while humbling has to do with the will. The bowed head and the bent knee are symbolic of human will surrendering to the will of the One we serve. Jesus bowed in obedience to the will of the Father in the supreme act of humility.

His acts of emptying and humbling were re-visited on several occasions. When Jesus was tempted—in the wilderness and on the cross—He had the ability to reclaim His rights as God and rise above the hurtful circumstances, but He chose to keep His hands open, releasing His rights for the sake of people and to fulfill His commitment to serve the Father's will. In the Garden of Gethsemane, Jesus' most intense struggle may not have been an aversion to physical pain, but a battle of the wills. In the supreme act of humility, Jesus said *No* to His own will and *Yes* to the will of the Father: "Nevertheless, not my will, but Thine be done!" (see Matt. 26:39).

This passage, perhaps more than any other, shows the pattern of the true servant leader. It demonstrates the core, the foundation, the motivation, the *identity* of the One whose ministry activities are the blueprint for our own. Overlooking His servant approach to those activities, however, makes void our ability to follow His blueprint, and attempting to replicate servant leadership as a style misses the power of the identity that propels it. *Identity* is where effectiveness in pastoral leadership comes from—not style, but condition.

One of the most important factors when considering Jesus as a servant leader is the question, Who was Jesus serving? To claim servanthood implies there is a master, and if you say you're a servant leader, you must first say *who* you are serving. Activities reflect the identity of the servant and—more important—the priority of the Master.

So, who was Jesus serving? Was He serving Himself? Likely not—the battle of wills in Gethsemane would not have been necessary if that were the case. Was He serving people? A case could be made that He was, because He did so many good things for people. In fact, Matthew records that Jesus said that He "came not to be served, but to serve" (Matt. 20:28). The word Jesus used here indicates *ministry* more than servanthood: He came not to be *ministered* to, but to *minister.* This helps us answer the question, Was it *servanthood* He gave to people, or *acts of service*? A huge difference.

Again, who was Jesus serving? The only appropriate answer, which Jesus Himself gave, is that He came to "serve the will of my Father."

He emptied and humbled Himself in order to serve the will of His Master. He wasn't trying to meet everybody's desires or needs; He wasn't trying to impose His own will and preference. He was simply serving God. Because the will of the Father was to restore people, Jesus' agenda was already set—it was up to Him to affirm His choice again and again, from His temptation in the desert to His death on the cross.

Who Are You Serving?

Servant leadership hinges on the question, Who are you serving? Most pastors would say that they serve their people. Is that really what Jesus did? He cured, He taught, He convicted, He disciplined, He blessed and He preached—but those were *acts of service* that ministered to the needs of people. Those acts sprang from His commitment to serve God's will for people to be restored. Jesus had one Master, not many. If you say that you serve people, you become a people-pleaser. That path leads to burnout and frustration when you can't meet everyone's needs. You wind up chasing an unattainable objective set for you by broken, hurting people, expecting you to meet every demand. If you fall prey to that trap, you become co-dependent with needy people, and miss the effective ministry of meeting their needs out of the quiet confidence of serving God.

There are many masters from which to choose. You may serve your own thirst for recognition or your desire to be secure—when you peel away the layers of ministry activity, you see that you are serving yourself. Perhaps you are serving the expectations of your parents, your peers or your overseers. You will strive to fulfill the will or wishes of your master, whoever or whatever that is. If your master is self, then self will impose the agenda. If your master is others, then their will and priorities will flavor your choices and behavior. If your Master is God, then your behavior and actions will reflect God's priorities and nature—

just like Jesus. A servant strives to please the master. Who is yours? Your master will determine:

1. *Who you become.* When your identity is tethered to a center, that center imprints itself on you. Servanthood, by definition, is yielding your rights and will to the master. This allows the master to work through you, to shape you and to transform you into who the master wills.

2. *What you do.* Every master has an agenda. Anyone who is pledged to serve the master will marshal his or her energy and efforts to fulfill that agenda. Your activities will bend to the agenda of whomever you serve.

3. *How you do what you do.* Serving a master is not only about "what" but also "how." Have you ever run into a Christian leader who is vocal about what he's doing and it all sounds good until you work with him and find him to be truly *un*-Christian in his demeanor? Some of the most hurtful people to the Church are not its sworn enemies, but those who do not reflect godliness when doing Christian activities. It is not possible to serve God without godliness becoming integrated into how you do your work.

Choose your master well. It is the most important choice you will make, and it will be the difference between effectiveness and ineffectiveness in pastoral leadership.

The Formation of the Servant Leader

Scripture is not only clear about what it means to be a servant leader after the example of Jesus, but it also shows us a pattern of formation for servant leaders. Take a look at Isaiah 52:13-15:

> See, my servant will act wisely; he will be raised and lifted up and highly exalted. Just as there were many who were appalled at him—his appearance was so disfigured beyond that of any man and his form marred beyond human likeness—so will he sprinkle many nations, and kings will shut their mouths because of him. For what they were not told, they will see, and what they have not heard, they will understand.

There are three stages of formation: Verse 13 is the stage of *declaration*, verse 14 is the stage of *suffering* and verse 15 is the stage of *fulfillment*. Let's take a walk through various accounts of leaders in the Bible and see the formation pattern of the servant mind-set that they all have in common. Note how this pattern becomes evident over the course of their lives.

Consider Jesus. At His baptism, God spoke and a dove descended with the *declaration*, "This is my Son" (Matt. 3:13-16). In His Passion, we find the *suffering* that resulted from His choice to serve the Father—the declaration of His identity was hammered out in reality. Then He rose from the dead and, in so doing, *fulfilled* all that God had willed for Him: to restore people to wholeness.

Or think about King David. When he was a boy, Samuel the prophet came and *declared* David to be the future king of Israel. It wasn't long, however, until David found himself running from cave to cave, scratching out a bare existence, fighting for his survival. Can you imagine the confusion in David's mind, having been anointed and celebrated as the next king and then finding himself *suffering* like a common criminal? Yet God called David "a man after my own heart" (see Acts 13:22). What greater *fulfillment* could one ask for?

Or what about Moses? He was born and raised in the courts of Pharoah, knowing that he would serve his people in some great way, having been *declared* a future leader. A few short years later, he was in despair, *suffering* 40 years of wilderness duty as a shepherd. Imagine his sense of loss, disillusionment and hopelessness. Then fast-forward to his meeting with God face to face on Mount Sinai. What *fulfillment* and confirmation!

Look at Esther. She was Queen of Persia when her cousin *declared* that God had made her Queen "for such a time as this" (4:14). She *suffered* the struggle of choosing between her own life or saving her people. And finally, the Jews' "sorrow was turned into joy and their mourning into a day of celebration" (9:22) when Esther *fulfilled* her calling to rescue them.

In the New Testament there are many examples of this formation pattern, Paul chief among them. Here was a man *declared* on the road to Damascus to be one whom God would use mightily, who *suffered* at the hands of those whom he once had served. Yet God affirmed Paul's calling to church leaders, and his mission to the Gentiles began the *fulfillment* of the Great Commission.

Name	Declaration	Suffering	Fulfillment
Jesus	Baptism	Crucifixion	Resurrection
David	Samuel's anointing	Cave dwelling	God's heart
Esther	Queen	Possibility of death	Jews saved
Paul	Damascus road	Persecution	Mission to Gentiles
You	_____	_____	_____

Now consider your own life and calling. Are you able to recall the moments or seasons of each stage? Let the events of your life tell their story and see if this pattern has emerged. Let the Holy Spirit guide your thinking. This is not a prescriptive formula; it is a *descriptive pattern* that seems to be evident in the lives of those leaders whom God has used with great effectiveness.

It's important to note that a person cannot proceed from *declaration* to *fulfillment* without passing through *suffering*. In fact, suffering is the unique feature of Kingdom leaders, fundamental to the formation of the servant identity. Without it, some other agenda is at work, likely that of self. This is not to say that we should run out and try to craft our own journey of suffering so that we can move on to fulfillment and exaltation! Suffering is not the goal; *it is the path*. It is not a prescription; it is a description of how God forms leaders, essential but not to be sought after or designed. Through suffering, self-determination is burned away for the will of our Master.[5]

The Calling of the Servant Leader

One of the greatest deterrents to the growth of the Church in recent years is the rise of uncertainty among its pastors. Effectiveness decreases in direct relation to the insecurity of pastoral identity. It's not surprising, given the pressure to obtain observable results. Pastors are like anyone else: They tend to perform where there is a clear expectation to perform.

As our church structures create systems that reward performance and expect objective results, pastors tilt to that expectation. Deep down, however, many pastors trying to perform well sense an internal disconnect between their performance and their calling. They are called to serve God and minister to people—that's the call they answered, yet they find themselves having to produce results that can be evaluated, rebuked or rewarded. Identity is confused, performance is paralyzed and effectiveness takes a nosedive. Nothing gets done well. Growth stagnates in the church and health deteriorates in the home because the pastor is busy trying to figure out how to get the numbers up.

Take a minute to center yourself, pastor. Quietly consider your calling. You are called by God, not the institution. You serve God, not people. You minister *to* people, and the institution provides a means to fulfill your calling to serve God and to minister to people with coherence, accountability, affirmation and agency.

If the question, "Who are you called to serve?" is not answered early and clearly, no amount of training, money, effort or goodwill can alter the patterns of ill health that will work their way into the fiber of your congregation. You imprint people with the nature that is in you because the Church is more than an organization—it is the organic Body of Christ, and your influence shapes its DNA. Effectiveness in pastoral leadership is rooted in an identity molded after the servant mind of Christ.

* * *

Whether you are a strong, directive leader or a low-key facilitator, whether you are a team-building coach or an empowering participator, whether you are a strategic thinker or an operational manager, you are called to effectiveness in leadership. Effective leadership starts with a servant-leader identity, shaped by the declaration of the Holy Spirit, fired in the kiln of Christlike suffering and fulfilled as you are used by the Father to restore people to health and wholeness.

John Wesley's Covenant Prayer

I am no longer my own, but Thine
Put me to what Thou wilt, rank me with whom Thou wilt.
Put me to doing, put me to suffering.
Let me be employed by Thee or laid aside for Thee,
exalted for Thee or brought low for Thee.
Let me be full, let me be empty.
Let me have all things, let me have nothing.
I freely and heartily yield all things to Thy pleasure and disposal.
And now, O glorious and blessed God,
Thou art mine, and I am Thine. So be it.
And the covenant which I have made on earth,
let it be ratified in heaven. Amen.

Notes

1. Robert Greenleaf, *Servant Leadership* (Mahawah, NJ: Paulist Press, 1977), p. 7.
2. The Greenleaf Center in Indianapolis, Indiana, is an excellent source of information regarding the expanding network of organizations and events centered on servant leadership, especially in secular environments and applications. See www.greenleaf.org.
3. For applications of the contemporary understanding of servant leadership, see *Servant First Reader*, edited by Grace Preedy Barnes (Indianapolis, IN: Precedent Press, 2006).
4. Philippians 2:5-11 is referred to as the *kenosis* passage because it describes the "emptying" of Jesus Christ of His "Godness" to be incarnated as a human.
5. An additional description of the pattern of formation is found in Kevin Mannoia, *The Integrity Factor* (Vancouver, B.C.: Regent College Publishing, 2006).

George Herbert lifted the subject of pastoral effectiveness to another level in his classic work *The Country Parson*. Herbert declared that he wrote to "set down the Form and Character of a true Pastor, that I may have a mark to aim at." Herbert addressed the characteristics of those whom he deemed effective pastors, speaking of the "dignity" and the "duty" of the parson. The parson was to live a disciplined life of commitment especially in "patience during afflictions" and "mortification in regard of lusts and affections."

Moral purity and the pastor's testimony were the focus of Herbert's practical guidelines for pastors, people who pursue knowledge, reading, prayer and the joy of preaching, and are excellent communicators, understanding both the Word and their audience. To Herbert, an effective pastor was a person of charity, courtesy, fatherly compassion and one who integrated his professional and personal life. Most of all, an effective pastor is authentic, not having an air about him, "but is himself wherever he is." Perhaps most important to Herbert was that ministry flowed out of identity and passion, nurtured through spiritual disciplines.

CHARACTERISTIC 7

MODEL OF HOLINESS:

Models and leads the congregation in the pursuit of personal and corporate holiness

At first we just swapped jokes in the dining room of the university. She asked me out first (we still agree on this), but we had already eaten together many times, talking and laughing. After that first date, we spent a lot of time together, studying in the library, out on dates and hanging around campus together.

I began to do things differently because I wanted to please her. I opened myself up to her influence. It's not an unusual story, but like any blossoming romance, it demonstrates the power of influence that one person has over another.

As we grew to know one another, there came a time when she began to feel free to exercise influence in other areas of my life. I'm not sure when it happened, but at some point she had access to my wardrobe—suddenly I began to dress differently. Some of my favorite clothes disappeared (that wasn't a bad thing) and my outfits began to look sharper and more coordinated. As she accompanied me on shopping trips, new and different clothes hung in my closet.

Even my taste buds were altered. Not particularly a fan of the delicate, subtle flavors of her Danish palate, I preferred the bold, strong aromas of garlic, heavy sauces and seasoning. I used to say that Danes like flavors that kiss you on the cheek, while Italians like flavors that hit you like a truck. Gradually, however, I began to appreciate the delicacies and nuances of Scandinavian cuisine.

I used to hardly notice the intricacies of a small flower, but today I may actually pause on a walk to admire God's creation. She has influenced me and I have changed.

You probably have your own stories. If you are married, remember when you were single—do you recall what you were like? Or if you're single, think about what you were like before you met your best friend. Doubtless your story is like mine—you have changed. Opening ourselves completely to another person changes us.

While my examples focus on behavior and appearance, being in close relationship with someone means that our very thinking patterns are influenced—our attitudes, our values and our priorities. All have been changed because we have allowed another person access to our lives, and that person's life has rubbed off on us. We are different for it. We have become a little bit like him or her.

In a similar fashion, the holiness of God seeps into our lives when we open ourselves to God. It happens slowly and subtly, and we hardly notice what's going on until we look back and see how we have changed. Holiness is innately a part of God's nature, so we can hardly expect to spend time with Him without being affected.

Understanding Holiness

Holiness is one of the most misunderstood themes in Christianity, yet it appears in the Scriptures on almost every page. As we dig into the Bible, however, it seems as though each time the idea is mentioned, a different word is used: holy, holiness, sanctification, purified, set apart, perfected—these are all attempts to show a dimension of God's holiness. If we attempt to find a single definition in the differences, we will miss the diversity and lack of clarity that best convey the *mystery* of holiness. It is larger than our ability to parse, dissect, analyze and contain.

Holiness is not easily reduced to a formula—neither is it a doctrine that can be acquired by study and mental assent. It is a *state of being* that flows out of the heart of God in a relationally transforming manner. And that transformation is not limited to a person or people. It includes all of what God first made whole.

Because it is a transformation that happens by God's remaking creation into a whole and healed condition, it requires a willingness on our part to be transformed. Transformation implies becoming something you are not, and that requires permission, an act of the will.

This permission takes the form of vulnerability, wherein we open our lives to the influencing effect of God to change us in a way that brings greater conformity to Christ. I had to expose myself, and still do, to the influence of my wife. That took vulnerability—only then did her influence have a transforming effect. Likewise, we must expose ourselves to God and the influence of God's character if the transforming effect of holiness will have effect. Vulnerability is a prerequisite to transformation into the likeness of God.

A New Wind of Holiness

For many years, the notion of personal and corporate holiness has often been dismissed as rigid—almost fanatical—legalism. Thankfully, many leaders recognize that fact. Even some within the historic Holiness Movement have begun to admit that, contrary to the Movement's beginnings with Spirit-led people transformed by God and compelled to act, holiness had devolved into a fear of contamination. They began to dialog about how the message of holiness and its transforming power had been commandeered by institutional hijacking that had eviscerated its impact on both individuals and communities.[1]

A wind began to blow and a cry for something more gave rise to the pursuit of holiness as *transformation*. Central to this new wind was a clear sense of passion, mission and fire that had been constrained by the bounded and shackled thinking of holiness as a set of behaviors to be mimicked. The center of gravity for the message began to move once again from the perimeter to the center: from behaviors to motives, from fear to love, from exclusion to inclusion, from spiritual compartmentalization to integrative wholeness.

Holiness as illustrative of the gospel is manifested on two fronts. It includes an internal dimension of transformation of the heart, mind and attitude to make one like Christ in motive and love. But it also includes an external dimension, wherein inner transformation results in compassion and engagement with others and the environment for the Kingdom's sake. There can be no personal holiness without social holiness. True inner transformation by the deep work of God's Spirit cannot be restricted to the inner life—it will play out naturally in our relationships with others, our community and our world.

Truly transformed people let their lives make a difference by engaging and responding to their surroundings, whether to injustice, social sin, human hurt, poor stewardship of resources or environment, or spiritual bankruptcy. Holiness brings wholeness and healing to broken creatures and creation in an effort to restore the image of God.[2]

Effective pastors embrace their influence as a holiness role model, demonstrating what living like Christ looks like in today's world. They place a priority on helping their congregation be increasingly transformed into Christlike people who bring wholeness to their surroundings.

Set Apart for Love

Through these various ebbs and flows of the Church over many decades, it's not hard to imagine how people, including pastors, have come to misunderstand what is meant by holiness—yet we cannot escape the reality that it is vital to effectiveness in ministry. The call to holiness has been one of the greatest factors in the growth of the Church around the world, but more important, it is the starting point for godly character in pastors. "Holiness" is not just another word for "piety"—it is the holy character of God transforming your life, resulting in an impulse to bring the wholeness of Christ to everyone and everything around you.

Holiness is not bondage and exclusivism—it is abundant life and freedom. Holiness is not living up to the rules—it is living beyond the rules in the fullness of God's image. Holiness is not retreating into isolation—it is engaging in love. The pursuit of holiness will never cease because love can never be exhausted. Holiness is *transformation* engaged in real life (it is relevant) and *otherness* transforming all that surrounds it (it is missional).

Many folks emphasize one or another dimension of holiness over the others and find themselves caught in the extremes. These extremes may be legitimate dimensions of holiness, but if they are not held in tandem with the others, they fail to capture the *wholeness* of the character of God. Holiness is often understood in polarities. For example, some understand holiness as *otherness*: God is Other, so we must be, too. Because they view holiness solely in this way, the idea of engaging with a broken, tainted world is repulsive: We must remain separate! But the healing power of holiness must not be kept separate from the people and creation for which God intends it—Jesus did not remain separate, and neither can we.

Inherently, holiness is relational. God, who is Person, expresses love for us, and in that love we are transformed. The essence of holiness is Christlikeness.[3] Because of this relational nature of holiness, it can only be appropriated in our lives through intimacy and vulnerability with God. Likewise, we can only become conduits for transforming holiness through relationships, which allow us to influence others' lives. John

Wesley described a life transformed by God's holiness like this: "We mean one in whom is the mind which was in Christ and who so walketh as Christ also walked . . . he loveth the Lord his God with all his heart, and serveth him with all his strength. He loveth his neighbor, every man, as himself; yea as Christ loveth us."[4]

Holiness by Osmosis

In Mark 3, we read about Jesus inviting the disciples to journey with Him up a mountain. There appears to have been no particular agenda—Scripture only says that He called them to "be with Him." To tarry in His presence. To hang out with Him. To abide with Him. Not to have a conference, not to have a class, not to write a book or do a seminar. Not even to have a strategy planning session. Just to *be with Him*!

Jesus understood how God created us: We become like the people we spend time with. When we spend a lot of time with someone, that person begins to rub off on us and to change us. That can be a change for the better or for the worse, depending on who that person is.

Remember how your spouse or best friend has changed you? Remember how my wife changed me? My clothes, my eating, my attitude are all different, and those are just the outer changes. Deep internal changes have also happened because of so many years together.

Think about your children or the children of people you know. On occasion you have probably restricted your child from playing with a friend because every time he or she comes home from playing with "Aaron down the street" or "Britney next door," your child is violent, crude, loud, brash or disobedient. After a while, you get the connection and tell your child that they can no longer play together. Why? Because you know that your child will become like the kids he or she plays with.

Or perhaps your teenager is way off course and far from God. It causes deep pain in your heart just to think about it. You gaze longingly at the vibrant church youth group and desire so much to have your child spend just a little time with kids like that. Why? Because you know that if your teenager did, the qualities of those in the youth group would eventually rub off on your son or daughter and help him or her back to healing.[5]

Imagine, then, how tarrying in the presence of God and nurturing a growing relationship with Jesus Christ will affect you! If being with a spouse (another human being) or a teen hanging around another group of teens (also human) can have such a transformational effect, imagine what happens when you hang out with God, the Holy One of the universe.

That will change you.

Although fully understanding it is beyond our ability, spending time in the presence of a God who is holy makes us holy as God is holy. It just happens, because we become like the people we spend time with. It's part of our God-given nature to be affected and transformed in close relationships where we make ourselves vulnerable. The holiness of God is absorbed through intimacy and a vulnerable relationship with God through Christ, who "rubs off on us."

Modeling Holiness

Modeling holiness is not about being a great example of righteous behavior or pious living—it is walking humbly with God in intimacy and being vulnerable to the effects of God's nature and priorities. It is spending time with God, knowing full well that God's holy character and holy priorities will become yours.

Although behaviors are not how holiness is appropriated in your life, they can certainly give you an indication of God's holiness (or lack thereof) at work in you. Where your life is held captive by behaviors that are not pleasing to God, you can be sure that the transformative nature of God is being interrupted in its work in you.

The nature of who you are in your character is dependent on the diet that feeds your heart. If your diet is the presence of a holy God, soon your life will reflect that. If you feed your soul the food of selfishness, obsession, achievement or control, however, soon your life will reflect the same. And hear this clearly: Having it both ways is not an option. In other words, you cannot hold the position of spiritual leader while feeding the appetites that result in selfishness or ungodliness. What do you feed your soul? What is the diet? What do you watch on TV? The Internet? In magazines? How do you invest your time? Where do you spend your money? Choose well, because all of these shape your nature, which expresses itself in holy or ungodly behaviors.

From your inner condition, you influence the people of your congregation, and eventually they will become like you. Remember, your people open themselves to your influence. They make themselves vulnerable to you—to your teaching, your counsel, your tender touch—and that vulnerability gives you tremendous influence, which is a sacred trust given by God and them. They will be affected by you, just as you are affected by those to whom you have made yourself vulnerable.

An effective pastor recognizes this influence—first of God on his life, and then of his life on the lives of the people. Gordon MacDonald describes the pastor who models holiness this way: "He/she is quite aware that they are often watched as they seek to emulate Christ."[6]

The River of Holiness

Rivers always move. A stopped river is no longer a river; it is something else. A river's movement is very like the holiness of God, and the refreshment we receive when we are "on the way." We are always becoming. Remember, the pursuit of holiness never ceases because love can never be exhausted. It is always fresh, dynamic, moving into new places to transform people and circumstances with the love of God.

Growing in grace and in deeper knowledge of God's holiness is part of the call to be a disciple, to say nothing of the call to serve God as a pastor. There can be no "stoppedness" in being a pastor. It is all about moving forward, journeying, becoming, penetrating and flowing, compelled by the holiness that pours from the heart of God.

Rivers always change. (Obviously, if a river is always moving, it must always be changing!) Rivers respond to their surroundings, carving new paths and flowing into new territory.

Our family has a favorite spot in Yosemite National Park. It is a place where the river flows rapidly to create many small islets—in fact, it's called Happy Isles. One year I walked with our youngest son as far as we could go on one of the isles and perched on a large rock to watch the water foam and cascade past us. I pointed out a particular tree that was hanging precariously over the edge of the river.

The next year we went back to Happy Isles, and my son and I took the same hike. But something was different. We couldn't find the rock, and the tree we had seen was no longer there. We stood as far upstream as we could, again admiring the power of the water and the freshness of the spray. All of the sudden, my son shouted and pointed to a large rock 50 feet farther upstream in the middle of the flow. Unmistakably, it was our rock from the previous year, but we couldn't get to it—the entire curve of the river had changed.

If you are averse to change in your life, the river of God's holiness is not for you. If you prefer the static condition of having arrived, you will be shocked at the perpetual journey that is inevitable in the pursuit of holiness. God's holy river, by nature, will change everything in its path—sometimes through joy and other times through pain—always for good in the fresh flow of holy transformation.

Rivers always bring life wherever they go. Have you ever seen satellite pictures of Earth? From far in space, the camera shows the stark desolation of the great Sahara Desert in North Africa, but along the eastern edge of that barren expanse is a thread of green winding its way from south to north to end at the Mediterranean Sea. The Nile River cuts a path through one of the harshest places on Earth. It brings the lush green color of life. People, animals and plants alike are drawn to its cool waters.

In similar fashion, the holy river of God brings life wherever it goes. Whether it is the brokenness of a soul in your care or the barrenness of your own life, there is hope and life where God's river flows. It flows into the desolation of the urban community around your church, or into the bleak affluence of your church's suburban neighborhood. It flows into barren deserts thirsty for the life-giving water of God's transforming holiness.

Ezekiel 47 records that the prophet was invited to enter a river flowing from the temple, which symbolized the holy presence of God. The river flowed through the desert of its surroundings, bringing life to all who would enter it. So Ezekiel did. First he went in ankle deep.

Perhaps you have accepted the invitation to step into the river. No question that your feet are in the water, but they are planted square-ly on solid dirt—*in* the river, but holding fast to your own destiny, cir-cumstances, performance and priorities. Have you noticed that when you stand in the edge of a fast-flowing river, the water begins to wash away the dirt from under your feet? When it erodes a bit too much, you lift your feet to plant them more securely on solid ground. Oh, there's no question you're in the river of God, but you're taking great care to stand firmly planted in your own agenda, destiny, priorities and plans.

Then there is an invitation to come deeper into the river. Ezekiel accepted and went deeper, and let's say you do, too. Now the flow of the river is strong, and you have to exert quite a lot of energy to keep stable and firmly planted in the dirt beneath your feet. But the river of God's holiness beckons, urges, presses you to a willful act of vulnerable surrender, to let go and let the holy character of God transform and carry you into wholeness and effective life and ministry.

When God invited Ezekiel farther in, the prophet remained planted—deeper in the water, to be sure, yet firmly fixed in the security of his own control. Will you stay with him, in the river but not *in* the river? You've been to Bible school or seminary. You've pastored for many years. You are admired and respected for your position. The imprint of your feet in the river bottom is clear and well established. You are in the river and everyone can see it—but your feet remain planted on solid dirt.

And then God says, "I want you deeper still. I want you in the middle where your feet can't touch the bottom!"

If you're anything like me, you find your feet scratching and scrabbling for a toe-hold of control as the water rises, just to keep your face above water so that you can breathe. On tip-toe, you do everything you can to keep yourself in control, not carried away by the flow, fighting it with every ounce of energy you have.

Finally, you can keep yourself upright no longer, and in a desperate act of release, your feet leave the bottom. You are no longer in control. Your feet are off the dirt. You are completely at the mercy of the river. You will either sink like a rock or be carried by the current.

That's when it dawns on you: This river is trustworthy! It will hold you up! The very thing you were fighting is what saves you. You can no longer touch bottom, and you're dependent on the river of God's holiness to transform you, hold you, carry you.

You also notice that you no longer fight against the current. You are carried by it and a quiet peace characterizes your life. Your energy is no longer expended trying to fight God by shaping your ministry in your own image or likeness.

You perceive that before, as long as your feet were holding you stationary and in your own control, you stood watching the river flow past, seeing the mighty works of God, but never part of them. Now you are carried by the river of God, watching as the world goes by. Your perspective has changed. Having become immersed in the river of God, you move in oneness with God's character, flowing in dynamic harmony, changing the landscape around you as part of the great flow of God's work in the world.

Later in chapter 47, Ezekiel was reminded that wherever the river goes, it brings life, life that drinks from the river of God and bears fruit. *That* is effectiveness. Sterility, anxiety and frustration accompany the pastor who stands in the river firmly planted in the dirt. Effectiveness, life, fruit and transformation are the natural result of pastoral living that is immersed in the holy river of God.

* * *

As we open ourselves in vulnerability to intimacy with God, our natures are transformed into God's holy nature, and our priorities are realigned with God's priorities for wholeness and healing for broken people and fractured creation. One is the inner transformation of our condition to become holy as God is holy—our nature. The other is the manifestation of that transformation as we fulfill God's mission of restoration in the world—our priorities.

Will you open yourself to the life-giving river of God's holiness, always moving and always changing as you are transformed by the presence of Christ?

Notes

1. "The Holiness Manifesto" released in February 2006 is a document written by representatives of 10 holiness denominations in an effort to rearticulate a contemporary understanding of holiness for the twenty-first century. At the core, the Manifesto establishes love as the center of holiness and God as the only source of love. From this, the heart of those who seek is transformed through deliverance from sin and self-centeredness in order to love and serve God and others, and to be stewards of creation. Visit www.holinessandunity.org for more information.

2. Theodore Runyon, in his book *The New Creation*, describes the salvation God offers as restoring God's image in creation, bringing people to the wholeness God intended.
3. Thomas Oord and Michael Lodahl have provided an explanation of the core of holiness and its relational nature in their book *Relational Holiness* (Kansas City, MO: Beacon Hill Press, 2006).
4. John Wesley, *A Plain Account of Christian Perfection* (Kansas City, MO: Beacon Hill Press, 1966).
5. Diane LeClerc, "Holiness: Sin's Anticipated Cure," a paper presented at the Wesleyan Holiness Study Project , May 2, 2005, in Azusa, CA, sets holiness as the means of healing for the effects of fallen creation. Available as a downloadable .pdf at http://holinessandunity.org/fs/index.php?id=796 (accessed February 2007).
6. Gordon MacDonald, written comments on the *15 Characteristics of Effective Pastors*.

First Peter 5:2-4 speaks directly to the *focus* of effective pastors:

> Be shepherds of God's flock that is under your care, serving as overseers—not because you must, but because you are willing, as God wants you to be; not greedy for money, but eager to serve; not lording it over those entrusted to you, but being examples to the flock. And when the Chief Shepherd appears, you will receive the crown of glory that will never fade away.

Though it may be a difficult concept to grasp, effective pastors understand the delicate nature of overseeing the church, resulting in an attitude of reflective brooding in private and never asserting itself in harsh or dominant ways in public.

Effective pastors are marked by compassion, not compulsion. They are not motivated by money, but by the opportunity to meet needs. They understand the necessity of leadership, but they refuse to misuse their position for personal privilege. True shepherds go first—they guide by example. Instead of driving the sheep, they *lead* the sheep.

PRAYER LIFE:

Models an effective, regular, growing prayer life

"Prayer is the key to growing your church!"

"If your church isn't growing, it's because you're not praying!"

A quick and unanimous "Amen" must be given to the idea that effective ministry flows from effective prayer, but for many pastors, statements like these hang around their necks like ill-fitting neckties. Even the most pragmatic, culturally relevant Christian leaders dare not disagree with such clear spiritual truth, but instead of prayer being a life-giving relationship that fortifies their lives and ministries, it becomes a means to image enhancement, a choking experience of spiritual duty. "Expert" pastors sell us a formula for how to "pray so your church will grow." Such pragmatism can turn the beauty of prayer into a burden.

The distance between prayer as a method and prayer as a lifestyle is deceptive—it's like the mirage that seems so near and satisfying, yet is never reached. When pastors treat prayer as a means to an end, it degenerates into self-serving spiritual speech that leaves them spiritually thirsty.

The pastor's prayer time often takes one of five forms:

1. *Be-good prayers*: "Lord, I'm trying to be a good boy/girl and do my duty for You."

2. *Bargaining prayers*: "Lord, I'm putting in my time here and I expect some results in return for this effort."

3. *Bellyache prayers*: "Lord, I'm here to tell You how I really feel about the deacon board and especially John Big-Yap."

4. *Bless-me prayers*: "Lord, I'm going to give You a 20-minute speech with words I've learned from someone who seems to get results from You."

5. *Battle-on prayers*: "Lord, I'm going to scream at some demons for the next hour to help me feel better about the spiritual scene in my church."

Such prayers lack power because they lack either authenticity or accuracy. They may soothe the conscience of a pastor who is trying hard, but they fail to bring genuine help to him or his church.

Effective pastors have moved beyond prayer as a means—they have grown beyond the emptiness of ritual. They model a life of effective, regular, growing prayer that is relational at its core and believe in the power of prayer to influence their lives, the life of the Church and the world around them. This life of prayer permeates all aspects of the pastor's private and public life.

Lifting Hands to Heaven

Pastor Harold Taves was stricken with polio at a young age. For the rest of his life, he was unable to lift his left arm more than a few inches. Harold was a simple man of faith who responded to God's call, and over the course of his life, was a pastor in a few small Midwestern towns.

Few people will remember his name, except for those who had the joy of being in one of his little churches. Harold was an effective pastor because he was a pastor who had tapped into a relationship with God through prayer.

People frequently came into the church office to find Harold in prayer, often at the altar with tears streaming down his face. To this day I can see him, his good arm extended toward heaven, lifting the burden of one of his people before the Lord.

This life of prayer sustained Harold through challenges and disappointments. It altered the spiritual atmosphere of the worship services. It changed homiletically weak sermons into curiously compelling insights that reverberated in the hearts of those who listened.

Although I don't remember one sermon he ever preached on prayer, Harold taught me to pray. His anticipation of what God could do through prayer lifted me above my pathetic process of giving a wish list to God. He and God were friends, and it showed in their conversations.

Effective pastors understand the priority, the power and the privilege of stretching out their entire being to God in prayer. As David cried out in Psalm 141:2, they long for their prayers to be pleasing to God: "May my prayer be set before you like incense; may the lifting up of my hands be like the evening sacrifice."

This picture of hands spread out to heaven carries with it a gripping engagement for the heart of the effective pastor. Paul knew the power of being a leader who lives with a hands-to-heaven approach. While writing to his son in the faith, he challenged all believers: "I want men everywhere to lift up holy hands in prayer, without anger or disputing" (1 Tim. 2:8).

Hands lifted to the sky are an almost universal sign of surrender, indicating "yieldedness" and the need for help. Understood in this way, lifted hands are the ultimate symbol for true prayer, which is predicated on self-surrender. It is empowered only by throwing oneself fully onto the mercy of God and then boldly requesting His assistance.

Pastor Moses is our instructive example of this characteristic. Exodus 17:11 says, "As long as Moses held up his hands, the Israelites were winning, but whenever he lowered his hands, the Amalekites were winning." Moses' staff was his emblem of leadership—it was the outward symbol of his call, authority and ability. As he lifted his staff to heaven in an act of dependency, surrender and intercession, victory for the people of God was connected to the act of Moses remaining in a posture of prayer—hands to heaven, leadership offered to God. There is something powerful and effective when a leader lifts hands to heaven on behalf of God's people.

This is the posture that effective pastors live in. One of the most powerful things a pastor can do for her church is to surrender herself to God in a relationship of prayer, interceding for the victory of her people. Prayer alone is not enough, but if you don't start and continue in prayer, whatever else you do will never be enough.

The hands-to-heaven mind-set is characterized by three dimensions of a thriving prayer life: Identity, Integration and Intervention. Effective pastors, in their own language and means, progress in these three dimensions of prayer.

Identity Prayer

Hands-to-heaven prayer opens us to the deep work of God of forming our hearts. Identity prayer reveals, shapes, secures and sustains the pastor. It invites the searchlight of the Holy Spirit in so that any sin lurking at the corners of our lives is exposed. Identity prayer is communion that reveals God's delight in us, God's fresh grace for the day and God's powerful presence within us. This is prayer that shapes not only our self-image but also our self-reality.

Identity prayer is summed up in the words of a fellow pastor who daily prayed, "Lord, put Your fingers deep into the clay of my life today. Shape me so that others see more of You in me today."

Lloyd Ogilvie was the one who introduced me to Identity prayer. At a college chapel, Ogilvie said, "Allow me to share my life's prayer with you: 'Lord, make my life as beautiful as it was when You first thought about me!' " To be shaped through prayer into the original design God intended is a journey that leads to increasing and true effectiveness.

In 1996, nearly 40,000 pastors gathered in the Superdome in Atlanta for the clergy event "Fan Into Flame." When veteran pastor Charles Swindoll stepped to the microphone, they were not prepared for his first sentence: "When God wants to use a person greatly, He crushes them deeply."

Swindoll went on to highlight the call of Isaiah, with all of its pain, surrender and power (see Isa. 6). The prophet was before the Lord when the revelation of his own uncleanness came crushing down on him—and he was completely undone. As he stayed before the Lord, however, his sinful lips were not only cleansed, but they were also changed, empowered and commissioned into ministry. Pastors have the same opportunity as Isaiah to be humbled before the Lord to see a fresh revelation of their God, themselves and their call.

Jacob had the quintessential prayer encounter when he wrestled with God through the night (see Gen. 32:22-32). Holding on to God in the middle of the night is never fun—and often causes a limp—but it is the kind of praying that has life-shaping power. From that day forward, Jacob was known as *Israel*, which means "he struggles with God."

Almost every pastor wants to be known as one of God's best, a significant influence, a real prince or princess of God. But who wants to limp? We want to avoid the painful shaping of our inner selves, yet wrestling through the night is the way we fall into the greatness that God calls us to. An effective, growing prayer life is one that moves us past our defenses, beyond our fears and deeper than our self-deception. The journey of "Jacob" to "Israel," from "deceiver" to "prevailer" can only be taken through Identity prayer.

This kind of prayer happens primarily in times of aloneness and especially in times of pain. We first confess all known sin and ask for the root of such sins to be revealed, which puts us in a position for deeper shaping. Then we wait in the presence of God with an ear tuned to His voice. We come as we are—no pretense, agenda, façade or guardedness. Openness, transparency and vulnerability invite engagement and intimacy with the Father.

Eighteenth-century mystic and poet Archbishop François Fénelon described prayer this way:

> Tell God all that is in your heart, as one unloads one's heart, its pleasures and its pains, to a dear friend. Tell God your troubles, that God may comfort you; tell God your joys, that God may sober them; tell God your longings, that God may purify them; tell God your dislikes, that God may help you conquer them; talk to God of your temptations, that God may shield you from them; show God the wounds of your heart, that God may heal them. If you thus pour out all your weaknesses, needs, troubles, there will be no lack of what to say. Talk out of the abundance of the heart, without consideration say just what you think. Blessed are they who attain to such familiar, unreserved intercourse with God.[1]

Many pastors have found that establishing an altar place is helpful. This is a sacred space conducive to helping you focus and listen, an environment that is dedicated to interacting with God over matters of life and ministry. My first such place was a closet under the basement stairs, where I positioned a kneeling pad, a bench, a Bible and a small lamp. I didn't go into that closet except to seek God. I expected God to meet me there. I can remember crying, laughing, singing, reading, confessing and listening at that altar. I envisioned the backside of those stairs leading heavenward to God's throne. Perhaps they did.

Identity prayer is not a monologue about my sin or needs. It is, instead, an active dialogue, with times of listening for the thoughts of

God. As we learn to hear the voice of the Spirit, we receive the communion that builds the interior resiliency that ministry demands. Henri Nouwen captured this necessity:

> Why is it so important that you are with God and God alone on the mountain top? It's important because it's the place in which you can listen to the voice of the One who calls you the beloved. To pray is to listen to the One who calls you "my beloved daughter," "my beloved son," "my beloved child."[2]

To pray is to let God's voice speak to the center of who you are—to your guts—and let it resound in your whole being.

How many pastors have their effectiveness undermined by giving too much weight to the words of their critics? Or by dwelling on the injustices of the ministry? How often does the burden of unreciprocated love hobble the spirit of the pastor? David knew this kind of heartache, and his response should become our testimony: "In return for my friendship they accuse me, but I am a man of prayer" (Ps. 109:4). His resiliency was nurtured through his dialogue with God. His identity was well-formed through a life of prayer.

Integrating Prayer

For prayer to shape a pastor's life and ministry, it must be woven into daily life. Prayer is not something the effective pastor does in order to prepare *for* the day—it is the means by which he or she travels *through* the day. Integrating prayer is a running conversation with God that begins on waking and ends on the pillow at night. It is conformity to Paul's admonition, "Don't worry about anything, instead pray about everything" (Phil. 4:6).

Prayer must be integrated into the moments of ministry and become the natural reflex to whatever the day hands us. The conversation with the staff member who shares a concern elicits a moment of prayer. Caller ID showing a board member on the line is met with prayer. The offering report, the nursery problem, the hospital visit, the lunch with a new attendee, the new volunteer for Sunday School, the website layout . . . are all tackled with an under-the-breath conversation with the Father.

Archbishop Fénelon understood integrated prayer when he wrote, "Accustom yourself gradually to carry prayer into all your daily occupation—speak, act, work in peace, as if you were in prayer, as indeed you ought to be."[3] He knew that this attitude of prayer has transforming power. Integrating prayer into the minutia of life brings a sense of significance, satisfaction and holiness to the most humdrum tasks of ministry.

Many pastors enter ministry with unrealistic expectations of world-changing influence and weeks filled with study, prayer and teaching. Upon arrival at their first post, however, they can relate to Brother Lawrence, the sixteenth-century monk who found that peeling potatoes and washing dirty dishes were the unsavory realities of his weekly ministry chores. Brother Lawrence complained for an entire decade before beginning to "practice the presence of God." Four centuries later, we are still buying his book.[4] Why? As Brother Lawrence himself said, "There is not in the world a kind of life more sweet and delightful than that of a continual conversation with God." Effectiveness is not measured by how fast a pastor can escape ministry tasks that seem below his expensive seminary training, but by how thoroughly he can integrate prayer into the unpleasant or mundane chores of ministry.

Integrating prayer ties the loose ends of ministry together—it gives some order to the chaos of ministry. It brings together seemingly unrelated events and identifies common threads so that spiritual understanding results. We lay the variety of puzzle pieces before God and say, "Lord, You make sense of it all."

Integrating prayer operates like a gyroscope, which is a device for maintaining orientation: It continuously revolves around every circumstance to keep the pastor centered and stabilized. When journeying in prayer, the pastor can keep his or her bearings while navigating the maze of ministry.

Intervening Prayer

The privilege of prayer is a delegated authority for the disciples of Jesus to interrupt the reign of evil and extend the kingdom of God. The ability of the pastor to change the spiritual atmosphere of a congregation or a community through prayer must never be underestimated.

When the spiritual leaders of the new Church in Jerusalem were confronted with the choice of administration or intercession, their priority was clear: "We will give our attention to prayer and the ministry of the word" (Acts 6:4). That intersection between the spirit of prayer and the truth of the Word is the sweet spot from which a pastor can truly *preach*. The power of a sermon arises from careful attention to both intervening prayer and accurate preparation of the Word.

The old cartoon showing a pastor on his knees in prayer and a secretary opening his door to say, "Good, I am glad you're not busy," is all too common. Either the church people have shaped their priorities around practical service instead of the spiritual power of intercession, or the pastor is too busy serving the church to spend time intervening in prayer. But the apostle James reminds us that "the prayers of a righteous man are powerful and effective" (Jas. 5:16). A prayer of faith impacts the spiritual realm in heaven and the reality on Earth, and results in increased effectiveness.

Pastors sometimes pray as thermometers instead of thermostats. Like thermometers, their prayers reflect the reality of life in their congregation—they praise God for what is or they complain to God about what is not. Thermostats, on the other hand, monitor the temperature *and intervene*. They draw on the power of the furnace to heat the room. They change the atmosphere.

One National Day of Prayer, I felt directed by the Holy Spirit to do something totally uncharacteristic of my usual pattern. A busy intersection near our urban church had been the site of four robbery-homicides over the previous year, and the Lord prompted me to spend the day prayer-walking that corner, carrying a sign that read "National Day of Prayer: Praying for Peace in our Neighborhood."

I got everything from honks of support to mock drive-by shootings, but I sensed the Spirit changing the atmosphere through my prayers and the prayers of others. A year later, three new businesses had opened, the closed business had reopened and there had not been even one robbery or murder. God lovingly chided me about my small faith that prayer could change the atmosphere of a street corner.

Intervening prayers that are effective emanate from a friendship with God, not from the ego of an aspiring pastor—it is out of Identity and Integrating prayers that effective Intervening prayers arise. As a son or daughter of God learns his or her identity and walks through his or her days in conversation with God, he or she is prepared to intervene with accuracy and boldness. He or she begins to pray in the name of Jesus instead of in the name of his or her own small-minded desires.

Abraham is a biblical model on this point. Abram had his identity transformed by God to Abraham, and had traveled without knowing where he was headed, yet walked with God as he went. Abraham and God were friends. It was out of this relationship that Abraham prayed his powerful prayers of intervention, actually bargaining with God for Sodom (see Gen. 18:16-32). Abraham stood in the gap for Sodom, negotiating a deal with God to spare the city if even 10 righteous people could be found there.

Effective pastors journey into friendship with God and learn to exercise the power of prayer to intervene on behalf of their people.

Their prayers push back principalities and powers, releasing spiritual gifts and blessings. Such a prayer life demonstrates beyond debate that the pastor's dependency rests on God instead of self.

Effective pastors call their community of faith to join them in wielding such a dynamic force, and their invitation rings with integrity because people know the pastor is praying in the closet before calling for them to prayer in the sanctuary. As the pastor models this priority on prayer and calls the congregation to follow, results attributable only to God begin to occur in ministry.

* * *

I remember asking God to heal Pastor Harold of his polio injury so that he could lift both of his hands to heaven in prayer. It never happened. But Harold had already taught me that my responsibility was not to figure God out, but simply to pray in faith, allowing God to shape my identity, walking with God throughout the highs and lows of my days and intervening on behalf of His people.

Harold was immersed in a life of prayer and it produced effective results: His churches never grew beyond 100 people—but of those 100, more than a dozen went into full-time ministry, influencing thousands for Christ.

Notes

1. James Mudge, "Fénelon the Mystic," 1906. Online version available at the Christian History Institute online. http://chi.gospelcom.net/pastwords/chl175.shcml (accessed February 2007).
2. Henri Nouwen, "Moving from Solitude to Community to Ministry," Leadership Journal, Spring 1995. Online version available at Fellowship Bible Church of Colorado Springs http://www.fbccs.org/resources/papers/soli_comm_mini.asp (accessed March 2007).
3. James Mudge, "Fénelon the Mystic," 1906.
4. Brother Lawrence, The Practice of the Presence of God (Boston, MA: Shambhala Publications, 2005).

FOUNDATIONS IN CHURCH HISTORY
RICHARD BAXTER (1615-1692)

Richard Baxter wrote one of the classic works that brought definition to pastoral work. When Baxter spoke of being a "reformed pastor," he meant *one renewed in zeal for the work of shepherding God's people.* In one sentence, Baxter effectively stated the essence of the pastor's vocation, revealing all of its dignity and severity: "We are seeking to uphold the world, to save it from the curse of God, to perfect the creation, to attain the ends of Christ's death, to save ourselves and others from damnation, to overcome the devil, and demolish his kingdom, to set up the kingdom of Christ, and to attain and help others to the kingdom of glory."

Baxter pressed his readers into a self-audit through questions that revealed his understanding of effectiveness. These inquiries are as relevant today as they were 400 years ago: Do I really serve God or myself? Do I seek to meet the needs of others or am I actually pursuing self-fulfillment or a life of ease? Is my teaching and preaching merely a showcase for my intellect and abilities or am I compelled to proclaim the message as Paul, who exclaimed "woe is me if I do not preach the gospel." Finally, am I a reformed pastor, being renewed daily by the Holy Spirit?

HOLY SPIRIT EMPOWERMENT:

Believes in the power of the Holy Spirit and expects the Holy Spirit to work in an ongoing way

It's called "burying the rail."

Sailing is boring when the wind isn't blowing. But when the wind is gusting, sailing is a daring, heart-pounding escapade. Sails hanging limp in the stillness become taut with power, and your pulse and adrenaline skyrocket. In sailing, you "bury the rail" when your boat catches so much wind that the deck is nearly vertical and the side of your boat is underwater—we're talking a rush of speed, power and adventure.

Sailing with no wind and sailing in strong wind are very different experiences. Without wind you still have the boat, the water, the sail and the rudder—but you have no motion, no thrill, no water splashing over the bow. With strong winds, your boat surges forward to fulfill the purpose it was created for.

The same is true of pastoring: Without the power of the Holy Spirit, ministry lacks momentum. Pastoring becomes a repetitious cycle of the mechanics of the job, with no expectation of any significant progress. But when the Holy Spirit is moving, unpredictable adventure permeates everything—there is a "God story" waiting around every corner.

Some pastors sit in the boat for 40 years and never feel the wind. They swab the deck, shine the rails, hoist the sails and never venture out of the harbor. But the wind seldom blows in the harbor . . . it blows strongest when you lose sight of land.

Effective pastors believe in the power of the Holy Spirit. This is not about being charismatic, liturgical or evangelical in orientation—it's a posture that a pastor takes toward herself, her ministry and the Third Person of the Trinity. This pastor sees herself as having no power to produce anything of spiritual value without the assistance of the Holy Spirit. She understands the reality of the spiritual realm and the necessity of spiritual power, and operates with a dependency on the Spirit's empowerment and intervention.

Not by Might, Not by Power

Pastor Zerubbabel's challenge was similar to that of pastors today: build a temple in the face of opposition and indifference. As a leader, it was easy to grow discouraged and disillusioned, but God gave Zerubbabel a vision of oil lamps and a word of explanation that was undeniably clear: "'Not by might nor by power, but by my Spirit,' says the LORD Almighty" (Zech. 4:6).

The way the Church is built has not changed. The means to overcome resistance and break through apathy is no different. These are still the work of a dynamic partnership between a willing pastor and the power of the Holy Spirit.

Jesus taught the same truth using grapevines instead of oil lamps.

I am the vine; you are the branches. If a man remains in me and I in him, he will bear much fruit; apart from me you can do nothing (John 15:5).

The Spirit of Jesus abides in us through invitation, surrender and faith—a daily, hourly yielding to the Spirit's presence keeps us remaining in the vine. As we draw our daily life from the Spirit, we are empowered to be effective for the Kingdom and we bear significant fruit.

The fruit Jesus speaks of here is in both character and ministry. The indwelling of His Spirit causes a change of life and character that is visible to those observing our lives. Jesus promised that His followers will receive a power that changes them—the Holy Spirit's presence will make them more loving, kind and patient and they will have boldness and courage that was not possible on their own. People would notice a difference in the lives of those who encountered the Holy Spirit.

But a lifestyle of abiding in Christ and walking in the Spirit also produces the fruit of ministry effectiveness, the evidence that the kingdom of God is among us. It is people converted to Christ, disciples nurtured, relationships healed, addictions broken, leaders raised up, individuals called to ministry, needs met, injustice confronted and healthy living established.

Let's be honest: Many pastors substitute learning, skills, personality or effort for reliance on the Holy Spirit's power. Jesus, however, was very clear—no abiding, no abundance. Without the Holy Spirit empowerment that comes from abiding with Christ, we can do nothing. We can be busy and do nice things for people without relying on the Spirit, but to have full Kingdom impact, the life of the Spirit must flow through us.

Two of the top-five advertising icons of the twentieth century are the Marlboro Man and the Energizer Bunny. The Marlboro Man is the epitome of the strong, self-sufficient and capable American. He relies on himself to survive alone on the vast, wild prairie and thinks deep thoughts while staring into a Montana sunset (and smoking). The Energizer Bunny is the pink bunny in sunglasses and blue sandals, beating a drum. Since 1989, the Bunny has been marching onward, showing up in unpredictable places and influencing the situation wherever he appears. His secret? *The battery inside.*

The apostle Paul would identify with the Energizer Bunny, not the Marlboro Man: "I will boast all the more gladly about my weaknesses, so that the power of Christ may rest on me" (2 Cor. 12:9). Many pastors, on the other hand, aspire to a Marlboro Man style of ministry—cool, smart, confident and together is the unspoken goal. Two Marlboro men, Wayne McLaren and David McLean, died of lung cancer, but the Energizer Bunny keeps on marching. He might look a little strange, but he keeps going! He reminds us that endurance is all about the inner power, not the outward persona. Trusting in self for the power to perform ministry is as deceptive as smoking—it may taste (or at least look) good, but it leads to death.

When our panel described an effective pastor as one who "believes in the power of the Holy Spirit," the focus was not on pneumatology. Belief starts with biblically grounded theology, but is habitually, powerfully applied to life and ministry. Effective pastors believe that Jesus' last promise while on Earth was a lasting promise and may still be claimed today. Acts 1:8 is the birthright of every follower of Christ and especially those who are leaders: "But you will receive power when the Holy Spirit comes upon you." Pastors with this characteristic exercise faith, expecting supernatural empowerment in their daily lives and the Holy Spirit's active work in the congregation and world around them. They know that the Holy Spirit's activity carries with it an internal personal dimension, as well as an external ministry dimension.

Five classic scriptural symbols for the Holy Spirit can help us to understand the integration of ministry and Spirit-empowerment. Each of these symbols is needed to develop a full understanding—an overemphasis on any one aspect can dilute the wholeness of the Spirit's work.

Symbol #1: The Dove

In Luke 3:22, at the inauguration of Jesus' public ministry, we read that the Holy Spirit descended upon Him in the form of a dove. Let's notice that no re-ascension is mentioned.

When the dove came down, Jesus was preparing to face the wolves and lions and Satan in His wilderness temptation. At first blush, it seems odd that God would send a dove to a man going into battle. It makes more sense, however, when one recognizes that the dove symbolizes God's presence, comfort, assurance and tenderness.

Effective pastors live in communion with the dove—they embrace by faith the reality of the Holy Spirit's presence. They draw on the reassurance of the Spirit's presence when they are questioning themselves in the face of the wolves of ministry, and they take comfort in the Spirit's tenderness when they are tempted or attacked.

A pastor was describing his ministry in a medium-sized church. He told me, "The board is against me, my wife is too fragile to listen, my friends are too busy to call and my critics have nothing but time and free cell minutes . . . but today the Holy Spirit is with me. I draw great comfort and assurance from knowing that. I am not alone, so I will move forward." He walked in communion with the dove.

Effective pastors walk in sensitivity to the Spirit. Ephesians 4:30 reminds us that careless talk can "grieve the Holy Spirit." The more attuned a pastor is to the Holy Spirit, the more consistently he can live in alignment with that influencing Presence. Some pastors think they can read a trashy novel, watch an off-color movie, gossip about a lay person, yell at the kids, overeat at the buffet and overcharge their credit card and the dove will simply look the other way. But the Holy Spirit is grieved and seeks to communicate that grief to the pastor—the question is whether or not the pastor is being sensitive enough to listen.

Symbol #2: Fire

John the Baptist's prophecy was that the Messiah would baptize His followers with the Holy Spirit and with fire (see Matt. 3:11). Undoubtedly the disciples were reminded of this on the day of Pentecost when tongues of flame danced over their heads. Paul also linked the Holy Spirit and fire: "Do not put out the Spirit's fire" (1 Thess. 5:19).

The Holy Spirit's presence creates a fire of passion, zeal and enthusiasm. I have frequently felt my zeal for ministry waning. Gritting my teeth, trying harder, faking it to make it, positive self-talk and mass consumption of the Word cannot reignite my fire, but as I allow the Holy Spirit deeper access in my life, there is a surge of internal passion that rises within me.

Christian Schwartz conducted international research that led to his book *Natural Church Development*.[1] He found that passionate spirituality was a nonnegotiable characteristic for healthy churches. Effective pastors model and create an environment where this passionate spirituality can flourish.

Enthusiasm seems to be at an all-time low in pastors these days. Ministries are often more about survival than conquest and celebration, yet the power of enthusiasm is vital to attract people to ministry. Many people work in passionless jobs and at so-so marriages, so when they find passion in an on-fire leader, it is magnetic, drawing people to its source in God.

Please don't mistake passion and enthusiasm for a silver bullet in your ministry effectiveness arsenal. Every pastor is wired differently and the fire kindled by the Holy Spirit may look different for each. The Spirit's fire is not merely a frothy, whipped-up zeal that is sappy and inauthentic. People will quickly see that for what it is—a manipulative tactic not based in reality. The fire of the Holy Spirit is deep. Its source is not you, but its fuel is your fully consumed soul. No matter what form your passion takes outwardly, others will recognize it as a deep work of the Spirit and be drawn to and warmed by it.

One cold day an Anglican bishop was preaching to a handful of people in a large cathedral while John Wesley stood outside in the cold, preaching to hundreds. The bishop could stand it no longer and came out to inquire how Wesley could draw such a crowd in the cold while the church stood empty. "I set myself on fire and people come to watch me burn," Wesley answered. Fire is contagious.

Fires of our own making are *not* Holy Spirit fire. The prophet Aaron's sons, Nadab and Abihu, found this out the hard way. They mixed their own personal blend of fire rather than God's, and the results were deadly. Their self-made fire was unacceptable (see Lev. 10:1). When we make our own fire by mixing passion without purity, zeal without humility or enthusiasm without knowledge, we kindle death instead of life. If we are zealous about our egos, plans and dreams instead of about God's Word and God's glory, we invite judgment into our lives.

We must not generate our own flame, but we can lay out the kindling—bowing ourselves before God, admitting our dryness, urgently begging to have fire. As an old revivalist pastor was known to say, "I was born in the fire and I can't live in the smoke." Some pastors are just fine with the smoke of good programs, nice sermons and tidy buildings—but smoke will not impact a culture that begs for consuming spiritual fire.

Symbol #3: Oil

We read in the Old Testament that when priests, kings or prophets were installed into their offices, oil was poured over their heads, signifying the authority and provision of the Holy Spirit being imparted to them. They were no longer "David the shepherd boy" or "Amos the fig picker"—they became "the anointed of the Lord."

The anointed were not dabbed with the oil, they were drenched in it. Oil was poured on the head until it ran down the beard and flowed onto the robe (see Ps. 133:2). There was an abundance of oil for whatever opportunities or challenges arose.

Acts 10:38 describes the ministry of Jesus in terms of anointing:

God anointed Jesus of Nazareth with the Holy Spirit and power
. . . he went around doing good and healing all who were under
the power of the devil, because God was with him.

Our ability to do the good works of God and break through the powers of darkness depends on this same abundant, powerful, healing Holy Spirit anointing.

Holy Spirit anointing is essential for pastors from all traditions. Effective pastors understand themselves as the anointed of the Lord and their self-image is informed by this truth. They hold positions of authority with bold confidence and dependent humility, and continually request God's anointing on their preaching, teaching, counseling, leading and praying.

What is vital to know about anointing is that it does not come at your whim. It is not a tool you pull out when you want it. It's intricately woven into your life, but its only source is God's Spirit—it is tied to your office and also to your heart. This combination makes it possible for God to join with you in your responsibility to effect supernatural outcomes that are obviously beyond your personal ability.

A pastor friend and I were sightseeing in Stratford-on-Avon when he saw one of his church members walking toward us, weeping. One minute we were talking about Shakespeare, and the next, his spirit was attuned to the unknown needs of the approaching woman. When she arrived, he took her hand and said, "Your daughter has just been diagnosed with cancer but the Lord is healing her."

Shocked, she stammered, "How did you know?" The sudden revelation from the Lord quickened her faith, and the next week her daughter was pronounced cancer-free. My pastor friend trusts in a daily anointing.

While that kind of manifestation of anointing is uncommon to most pastors, walking in the Spirit should be common, with an expectation that unexpected ministry opportunities will take place. As God's anointed one, I live expectantly. Unanticipated conversations, unforeseen chances to pray, surprising openings to share biblical truth, unpredicted encounters with the poor—these are open doors for me to operate as the anointed of the Lord.

After a worship service recently, a homeless woman approached me with two young girls. I didn't have anything supernatural to say to her, but in the next hour as my wife and I fed her, paid for Motel 6 and loved on her little family, I felt as if oil was dripping from my fingers. My sermon that evening had been mediocre, but for the hour that followed the service, I was anointed. Her tears of gratitude were genuine, and I sensed the Holy Spirit speak through the Motel 6 security guard: "She's a good woman. You helped the right one tonight."

Effective pastors also believe that anointing is available for the people they lead. All 120 in the upper room at Pentecost—not just the apostles—received the Holy Spirit, and the New Testament teachings regarding the priesthood of all believers emphasize that anointing is available to all.

Pastors who recognize that anointing is not reserved for the clergy have more productive ministries because they open opportunities for ministry to everyone in the church, not just the ones on payroll. The resulting environment of interdependence and empowerment allows for a healthy, biblically functioning community as the presence of the Holy Spirit brings spiritual gifts to both the pastor and the people. When spiritual gifts are emphasized, believers sense their destinies—and as they use their gifts, they have moments of personal revelation where they sense anointing upon their lives. And once they experience anointing, it's not difficult to motivate people to continue using their spiritual gifts to build the Body of Christ.

Symbol #4: Wind

There are two ways to fly a kite. You can run really hard and let out a little string as you go, but the kite won't fly very high and won't stay up very long unless you keep running. Or you can search until you find a place where the wind is blowing, hold up the kite, let out the string and watch as it soars higher and higher.

In both Hebrew and Greek, the word for "spirit" (*ruach* and *pneuma*, respectively) means "breath" or "wind." Jesus linked the wind and the Spirit and asserted that they both blow wherever they please. "You hear its sound, but you cannot tell where it comes from or where it is going" (John 3:8).

Jesus later told His disciples (in essence): "Go into the entire world, but first wait for the wind. Let it carry you and your ministry to whomever I send you" (see Acts 1:4-5). The disciples must have been struck by the similarity when they experienced the "sound like the blowing of a violent wind" (Acts 2:2) on the day of Pentecost. The same wind still blows.

Here's an invitation: Don't use method number one to fly the kite of ministry, running hard and letting out tiny bits of string. Believe that the Holy Spirit is blowing and—as Henry Blackaby writes—"find where God is moving and join Him there."[2] The Holy Spirit will direct pastoral ministry if you will submerge your ego to the will of God. It is not always easy. The personal desire for external success will always be a distracting noise that may hinder your ability to hear the Spirit.

Remember the classic story? A Native American who had spent his life in the forest was walking down a busy Manhattan sidewalk with a businessman when suddenly he said, "I hear a cricket."

"I don't hear anything," the businessman responded. "There's no way you could hear a cricket in the midst of this traffic and all this noise."

The Native American replied, "Oh, but I do hear one." He continued to listen carefully as he walked to a small planter and picked up a cricket.

"That's amazing," exclaimed the businessman.

"Not really," came the reply. "It depends on what you're listening for."

With that, he dropped some coins on the sidewalk. Immediately, several people stopped and looked down.

Pastors may allow their ear to be tuned to the noise of the world—a board member, a wealthy donor, the latest celebrity pastor or even the needy around them. Or the noise could be internal—pride, ego, insecurities or fears. If the noise pollution of all these sounds is the only thing filling the pastor's ears, the ability to hear the Holy Spirit will become dulled until the still, small voice of God is ultimately drowned out. We must tune our ears to hear the gentle blowing of God's Spirit—if we are listening for Him, even uptown traffic at 5:30 P.M. won't matter.

Expect the Holy Spirit to blow across the congregation as you deliver God's Word. Watch for conviction, encouragement, love and hope to waft through the room as you preach. Actively trust the Holy Spirit to interpret your words and individualize your content to each person's heart, and never be surprised when someone says, "It was like you were talking just to me!" Have faith that the Holy Spirit will move through worship, sacrament, prayers and community outreach.

There are two kinds of expectation. One is an expectation that comes from *intimacy*, which springs from your familiarity with another's patterns of behavior. For example, I expect my daughter to make friends with everyone she meets because I have watched her do it a thousand times. I know her intimately and have grown familiar with her patterns.

The other kind of expectation comes from *personal demand*, which proceeds from a self-initiated effort to control or shape things to a particular outcome. Let's say, for example, that I expect the new Sunday School leader to recruit several new teachers—not because I know him and his gift for recruitment, but because it's what I want him to do and what will make me look better as a pastor.

The Holy Spirit will move—not when we demand Him to do so, but when we draw close and become intimate with God's Spirit. Effective pastors come to anticipate and depend on the Spirit to cause unpredictable works to happen because they have become intimate.

The adventure of this dependence on the Holy Spirit is that you don't know where the wind will take you. It may be blowing you somewhere in your ministry you never anticipated. It took Pastor Joe to the affluent agnostics, Pastor Brenda to the addicted, Pastor Jack to the suburbs, Pastor Brad to the coffee shops and Pastor Lyn to the inner city. It took Pastor George to liturgy, Pastor Tim to spontaneous worship, Pastor Debra to seeker-friendliness and Pastor David to signs and wonders. You don't know where it is going, but when you're Holy Spirit-empowered, you listen for the breeze and follow when it comes.

After eight years of rapid growth, our local church was facing a dilemma. With 700 attendees and only 40 parking spaces in our urban setting, we had to either relocate or reengineer the church—so my wife and I went away to listen for the breeze. We reasoned that we could relocate and build a megachurch, but the Spirit said something different. The wind blew another direction. We sensed the Spirit directing us to stay put, reorient the church and send out groups of people to plant churches in our area and beyond. Seven years and several new churches later, we are convinced that we heard the Holy Spirit.

We can't force the wind to blow, but we can hoist the sails of surrender, faith and openness to catch more of the breeze when it blows, and we can expect the Spirit to move—sometimes in gale-force gusts, sometimes in gentle breezes, but always moving.

Symbol #5: Living Water

In a semi-arid land like Palestine, the supply of water determines the degree of life. Where there is plentiful water, there is an abundance of life. Livestock, plants and people multiply and flourish. Natural springs are limited in supply, however, and before modern water technology, thirst and dryness and emptiness were common.

Living in a twenty-first-century culture that has 10 brands of bottled water at every 7-Eleven, we might fail to appreciate the reality of thirst and the joy of water. But in Jesus' day, water was a matter of life and death. Jesus stood up and shouted:

> "If anyone is thirsty, let him come to me and drink. Whoever believes in me, as the Scripture has said, streams of living water will flow from within him." By this he meant the Spirit (John 7:37-39).

An effective pastor knows how dry people really are. He also knows how dry he can become himself—without the spring of the Spirit, he doesn't have any water to offer. He also knows that this living water is available, real and never-ending, and he faithfully guides his people to that spring.

Ministry can only be done effectively if pastors are willing to pour out our lives like the drink offering poured out before the Lord in the temple (see Lev. 23). In biblical pastoral leadership, we do not just offer the gospel message—we pour out our own lives (see 1 Thess. 2:8). The problem with pouring out is that it leaves us empty, and unless we have a dependable "rewatering" source, we remain empty.

Jesus gave the solution for this ministry dilemma: a spiritual water cycle. Admit your recurring thirst, come to the right spring, be filled by drinking deeply and then be poured out again. The cycle is interrupted when a thirsty pastor seeks to fill himself with a substitute for the Holy Spirit. Escaping ministry dryness through activities such as hobbies, movies, books, traveling and shopping will never meet the pastor's true need. These activities are enjoyable and part of a full and joyous life, but they cannot address the thirst of the spirit. Replenishment from the drain of ministry is found only in continually drinking from the source of living water. Eugene Petersen captures this in his rendering of Ephesians 5:18: "Drink the Spirit of God, huge draughts of him" (*THE MESSAGE*).

*   *   *

When I started sailing, I was insecure about the wind. Being a novice sailor, my priority was keeping the boat level—I wanted a light wind so that I could put up a little sail to move slowly and safely along. My pro-sailing friend, Karl, taught me that the *real* adventure of sailing requires having faith and taking a risk. Sailing with Karl was like flying: We sliced through the water with great power, propelled by taut sails catching all the wind they could hold.

Pastors who thrive stop sailing their ministries at the speed of security and dare to believe that the Holy Spirit has the power to blow them where He wills. Pastors who move at the speed of the Spirit take risks to extend the Kingdom. Daily they invite the dove, the oil, the fire, the wind and the living water of the Holy Spirit to descend on, anoint, inflame, propel and fill their lives and ministry.

Notes
1. Christian A. Schwartz, *Natural Church Development: A Guide to Eight Essential Qualities of Healthy Churches* (Saint Charles, IL: ChurchSmart Resources, 1996).
2. Henry T. Blackaby and Claude V. King, *Experiencing God: How to Live the Full Adventure of Knowing and Doing the Will of God* (Nashville, TN: Broadman and Holman, 1994), p. 70.

Paul's instruction to Timothy and Titus gives us the most succinct description of the qualifications of pastors. In the diversity of the Church today, not everyone uses the same terms, but it is clear that these passages include people we are talking about: pastors.

The emphasis of the Titus and Timothy passages is on the *character* of the pastor. They are people with high moral convictions, emotional maturity, relational wisdom and spiritual balance.

When inspiring her class to write better essays, our English teacher would ask, "Would you be willing to distribute copies of this to your friends?" Pastors aren't perfect, but they need to be people worthy of being copied. Paul defined this pattern with an invitation to "Follow me as I follow Christ" (1 Cor. 11:1).

Paul's letters to Timothy and Titus are known as the Pastoral Epistles because of their emphasis on how to carry out the office of pastor effectively. These epistles indicate that Paul was primarily concerned with the teaching dimension. Pastors are to oppose false teaching (see 1 Tim. 1:3-7; 4:1-3) and to "command and teach these things" and to "be devoted to the public reading of Scripture, to preaching and to teaching" (1 Tim. 4:11,13). They are to "teach the older men," "teach the older women," "teach what is good," "encourage the young" and "teach slaves" (Titus 2:2,3,6,9). In teaching, the leader is to "show integrity, seriousness, and soundness of speech" (Titus 2:7-8). Paul underscores the elements of inner character, modeling and teaching as fundamental to the office.

INSPIRED PREACHING:

*Exhibits an ability to preach God's Word
in a fresh, invigorating way*

It ended like any normal weekly staff meeting. I was encouraged that our
church had grown to the point where I was able to hire a pastor to begin
developing a core group of people to plant a new church in a nearby
community. For the time being, he was working in our congregation to
build relationships, disciple the core group and lay plans for the launch
of the new church.

David was an evangelist. He was intensely focused on starting a new
church and was passionately investing in the ones he'd identified from
our congregation to serve as his leaders. He met with them regularly
and was leading them on a deepening path of commitment to Christ,
knowing that he would need these folks to be strong and healthy in
their walk with God in order to be successful in the new plant. He wanted to take full advantage of every opportunity to deepen them in their
faith, including Sunday services and the weekly message.

At the close of the staff meeting, David hung back and obviously
wanted to talk with me, which wasn't unusual. We had developed a close
relationship in our common commitment to church planting and winning people to Christ. As we stood near the conference room doors, he
seemed a little uncomfortable.

"That was a good message Sunday. Nicely organized and good
content . . ."

How nice, I thought. *It must have meant something special to him.* It was a good message. I had invested time and felt good about it, believing that it was truly what the people needed that week.

"But where was the *power*?!" David's intensity was one of his strong points, but right now his eyes felt like daggers.

What? How can he even say that?

It was my first church and the affirmation had been frequent. The people had responded well to me and expressed regular appreciation for my preaching over the three years since my coming. Now, out of the blue, this new friend was rocking my confidence.

I knew David was my ally—he truly desired to see me do well in my calling. But his core planting group was feeding regularly on the menu of messages I was preaching, and he needed them to be well nourished for the new journey ahead.

As I thought about David's challenge, I realized that preaching is not about a well-oiled structure or a smooth delivery or a nicely exegeted framework. It's not even about a theologically sound foundation. Preaching is about *effect.* I don't mean manipulated outcomes or emotional responses or intellectual assent—I'm talking about an internal effect that occurs in the souls of people and that draws them deeper in their walks with Jesus. At times it may be through intellect. At other times through emotion. At others, through deep reflection. And at others, through spontaneous action.

Preaching is designed to bring a breath of energy from God through God's Word and Spirit into the lives of hearers in a way that yields response.

I had forgotten the center of gravity for preaching. Sure, I'd been trained well. I did well in homiletics. I practiced good hermeneutics. I had a commitment to mission. But the preaching itself had become the focus, not the effect in the souls of the hearers. Preaching had become a skill I was honing so that my people would appreciate me.

Once preaching is disconnected from the effect in people, it becomes a fancy activity that we polish and perfect to gain public appreciation.

But David's challenge brought me up short. It called me to reevaluate what preaching is and where the power comes from. The need for transformational effect in people is one of the two primary power sources—the other is the deep work of God in the preacher to become a "vessel meet for the Master's use" (2 Tim. 2:21, *KJV*).

From that time on, I've been on a journey of discovering preaching not as an art to be appreciated in its own right, but as a means to effect the work of God in the lives of those who hear. Preaching is food that nourishes the souls of people, so it must be healthy and well-prepared— but mostly it must be full of power that provokes the gradual but necessary transformation of those who feed on it.

Bringing Supplies to Hungry Souls

Effective pastors communicate God's Word in ways that connect truth with the daily questions and needs of people. They grasp equally the condition of the listeners, the creativity of communication and the transforming power of the Scriptures.

Now more than ever, people are longing for effective and inspired preaching. It has become a determining factor in many churches of whether or not a pastor is called—it is the quality most often used as a primary point of evaluation. Few churches today will even consider calling a new pastor without having heard her or him preach, an exercise that is certainly open to abuse. It might be tempting for people in the search process to be captivated by talent, methods and personality or enamored by a great communicator, and miss significant signs of incompatibility or weakness of character.

Among the top 15 characteristics of effective pastors, this is one that at first glance appears to be in the realm of performance—in other words, it is a top-of-the-iceberg activity compared to a bottom-of-the-iceberg condition. Most of the 15 characteristics deal with an inner dimension or condition of the pastor, while preaching has an obvious tilt toward activity. Because of this tilt, it's important to beware of using preaching as a lever of manipulation to accomplish your own desire and agenda.

Preaching, as a characteristic of effective pastors, is not to be confused with teaching. Although there is a tendency to consider preaching as equivalent to teaching, it *is* different. Whereas teaching is focused primarily on the cognitive dimension of the hearer's life, preaching must be targeted *at the hearer's will* by means of the cognitive, emotional and behavioral dimensions of a person. It is a call to be different or to take steps of obedience to God.

Think of it this way: Imagine that a large pile of cargo needs to be transported from one side of a river to the other—from the heart of God to the hearts of your people. Teaching is like using a barge to get cargo across the river. A barge is flat-fronted and slow, but it carries a lot of cargo all at once, which may mean fewer trips to carry a huge load across. Upon arrival on the other side, the cargo is offloaded and stacked nicely for use later as it becomes necessary. It may not be unpacked right away and may sit idle and unused for quite a while.

Alternatively, preaching is like using a speedboat. It's fast and has a pointed front that cuts through the water with precision and speed, but it carries only a little cargo at a time. It requires many trips, each carrying a small but specialized item that can be quickly off-loaded and immediately appropriated to the need.

The driver of the speedboat must be keenly aware of the needs on the far side of the river in order to deliver the proper supply from the source—in effect, the preacher needs one foot in heaven and one foot on Earth, and a vigilant eye on the people's condition. Remember, preaching is not about your agenda; it's about finding the right nourishment and refreshment for their souls. This is the responsibility of the shepherd, and it demands that you preach from abundance and to effect.

Embodied Preaching

Inspired preaching is focused, creative, life-giving, rich and connected—to God and to people. This leads to a principle of preaching that cannot be underscored enough: *Preaching must be incarnational*—that is, it must be lived out in the life of the preacher. Does that mean that you must first experience everything you preach? Of course not. Preaching on sin does not mean you must experience as much sin as possible in order to speak effectively about it, but it does mean that you journey with your people as another person who stands in the need of grace. You must embody God's message before you speak it.

When God considered how best to communicate with us to restore the divine image in us, He attempted various ways—prophets, priests, kings, judges—but Hebrews says that "in these last days he has spoken through his Son" (Heb. 1:2). Jesus became God Incarnate to communicate God's message of salvation and healing. Were it not for the Incarnation, the Word could not have been heard to transformational effect. Jesus walked in our shoes so that we could be changed.

In like manner, you must be an incarnational word to the people, walking in their shoes as only a pastor can. Life must be the context of preaching. Only out of an abundance of relationship and trust will preaching be meaningful for the health and salvation of people. *Being* the message is as important as *speaking* it. People watch *and* listen—they don't just hear your words; they follow your example.

Fresh and invigorating preaching will come from within you to whatever extent you live the new discoveries of God's Word made real in your life. Embodying the message will convey it in a way that is life-giving and connects with the needs of people. Preaching is not a technique that must be mastered, not a craft to be acquired. Preaching is the fleshed-out reality of your calling to lead people to deeper love and knowledge of God. The incarnational nature of preaching means that God cannot do through you what God has not yet done in you.

That having been said, you should not feel a license to shoddy preaching. The truths you convey may be changeless, but the delivery must tap into both the creativity that comes from God and your passion for relationship with your people. You should always be asking whether or not your preaching is finding its intended impact—this is a good indicator of your effectiveness—and how you can better convey God's Word to your people. How will they hear you best? What will they most connect with? These stylistic questions cannot displace the fundamental message as the priority, but they should be factors for creating inspired preaching that is from God and connected to the people.

* * *

Whether preaching is topical, exegetical or expository is immaterial. Go with your preference and whichever will meet the urgent needs in your congregation. In any case, be sure that you rightly handle the Scriptures: Expose God's Word; don't force it or impose your agenda on it. God has communicated all we need for truth and life through the Word—finding context and structure is up to you through study and reflection.

The Scriptures will not fail to accomplish what God intends for them to accomplish—they are inspired by God and confirmed by millennia of wise and prayerful Christians as the prime source of authority for truth and life. Don't assume that you can improve or alter the Scriptures by shaping them to suit your priorities.

Your ability to preach in a fresh, invigorating way will be a marker both of your own vibrancy as an instrument of God and of your effectiveness in leading your people to be God's people. This is a task you must treat with great humility and surrender, and approach with passion and boldness.

John Wesley emphasized empowerment as a hallmark of effectiveness. Three primary categories of characteristics guided what Wesley looked for in pastors: graces, gifts and fruit. These three categories shaped the examination questions that Methodist pastors were asked annually.

Grace deals with the personal relationship the pastor has with God. Does the pastor know the forgiveness and holiness of God? Does he desire and seek nothing but God? Is he seeking God's holiness in his daily life? This category addresses the authenticity and vibrancy of the pastor's faith.

SURE CALLING:

Lives and ministers out of a clear sense of calling

"God told me to!"

It's the unassailable trump card used to justify so many things, good and bad. How can you argue with it? There is no defense, no argument. It silences all doubt and turns away questions from would-be doubters. After all, "Who am I to question what God is doing in her life?"

You must have heard it a thousand times. Perhaps you've even been confronted with people in your church who defy your efforts to guide, redirect or even stop action that may be detrimental by using the "God told me to!" argument.

Pastors seeking licensure and ordination can be especially prone to tossing out this phrase in the examination and interview process. Would-be pastors are asked about their reasons for wanting to be ordained, move to a new role or initiate some ministry, and the examination board is stymied when the candidate uses the trump card: "Well, all I know is that God called me."

Maybe you were one who confronted your ordination process with this ace up your sleeve to ensure that you got what you wanted—and now, perhaps, you're wondering if you were ever called at all. Maybe as you look around you see incomplete dreams, unresolved conflict, static, and plateaued ministry that require all the energy you can muster just to get up in the morning.

Effectiveness eludes you and you're beginning to wonder if what you thought was a call from God to be a pastor—or to pastor this particular church—wasn't a call at all. Maybe it was your own need or desire to live up to your expectations of what a pastor should be. Maybe you were trying to meet the desires of your parents and you described it as a call. Maybe you were trying to find your way into a position of power and influence, or to fulfill a misunderstood passion to help people.

Intricately intertwined with the effectiveness of pastoral leaders is the complex power of the call of God to serve. Sometimes something else is mislabeled as a calling when in fact it is not. Personal interest? Maybe. Desire to do something good? Probably. But a call from God to pastor? Perhaps not. Because calling is such an ongoing source of effectiveness, it's important to keep it clear and sure.

Effective pastors have a deep conviction that their work is an obedient response to God's divine purpose for their lives. They pursue ministry with an urgency, quality and tenacity that portrays God's grip on their souls.

Continual Call

A call from God to serve in ministry leadership is not static; it is dynamic. Calling does not happen once—it is renewed in vigorous engagement with day-to-day ministry opportunities. It is important to remember the time and place that you first sensed God calling you to pastoral ministry, but that event cannot be the source of motivation or power for your current ministry leadership. That's like trying to save daily manna for a rainy day! It rots and loses power. It's only when your call regularly informs and shapes your life that it is truly fulfilled.

Because of this dynamic relationship, your activities are motivated by your call, but your call is also affected by your activities—daily ministry reflection and action are the fertilizer that gives your calling life and support. The converse is also possible. You may begin with a healthy understanding of your call only to find that after years of ministry, your calling begins to be redefined to suit your need or desire at the moment. Either way—by keeping it isolated in the past, or by letting it drift over the years—your call can become diffused and eventually fade. But without it, your focus, motivation and source of fulfillment are gone.

Revisiting the nature and foundation of your call is an essential element to ongoing effectiveness in pastoral ministry because your experience and gifts are continually refined and developed to new levels. Your calling is shaped and molded each day as you recognize that in doing the activities of pastoral ministry, you are not doing so to please people, but to serve and please God. You live for One, not many. As Os Guinness has said, "A life listening to the decisive call of God is a life lived before one audience that trumps all others—the Audience of One."[1]

Absolute Call

God calls and the Church confirms. The Church is the Body of Christ. It is intended to work in coordination with and to fulfill the will of the Head. When someone appeals to a calling from the Head without commensurate confirmation of the Body, that calling is void. Jesus established the Church to carry out His will in the world, including multiplying new leaders.

Most denominations have a process for recognizing and affirming that call. It may seem cumbersome and meaningless, but any process can be meaningful if the attitude with which it is approached sees it as the work of the Church in confirming the call of God. The process is not simply a lot of hoops to jump through just to get a piece of paper on the wall—recognition is not a license to practice. It is an acknowledgment of what God is doing.

In guiding many ordinands as they prepared for their ordination service, I often had trouble describing the nature and import of this deep and mystical formation. It comes from a call and is confirmed by the Church in the ordination vows. I usually told them that there is a deep work of God that is manifested in them when hands are placed on them and the weight of their calling is confirmed by the Church. Their responsibility was to embrace that call and discover its fullness in complete availability to God. Countless times they came back later and testified, "I didn't know what you meant at the time, but I know what you mean now."

In any discussion of calling, it is imperative that there be clarity regarding what that means. So many things fall under the concept of calling that it would be easy to become confused—if not frustrated—simply out of confusion. Generally, in discussing the idea of calling in pastoral ministry, we refer to the type of call most reminiscent of Levi's call to serve God by spiritually ministering to the people. That Levitical call is all-consuming and redirects one's life completely in appropriating energy, gifts, priorities and even resources.

Notice in the accounts of the Exodus when Moses assigned each tribe to a place, Levi was left without. The Levites were assigned to the tabernacle and to bring its presence to the people wherever they were.

Likewise, when Joshua allocated land to the various tribes, Levi was given none. The Temple was their place, bringing the presence of God to the people and representing the people to God. Although they had a geographic place, it was so only to the degree that that place represented God among them.

In both cases, notice the importance of place, and see the close correlation between God's called ones and the absence of any attachments other than those closely associated with God's presence. In similar fashion, when we speak of the "call to pastoral ministry," there is a sense in which that calling transcends place and is free from any of the attachments that prevent complete loyalty and mobility to bring ministry to the people, wherever they are.

In the Methodist tradition of pastoral appointments, there is the assumption that once a person responds to the call of God to pastoral ministry, that person is committed to itinerancy. In other words, he is willing to go wherever it is necessary to fulfill his call and serve God and the Church. The old Methodist circuit riders emphasized this concept in their field preaching and rotating assignments of pastoral care that constituted their "circuit" of congregations.

The old-time Methodist pastor was completely dependent on the congregations for provisions. Remember how the priests in the Old Testament relied on the offerings of the worshipers to provide their livelihood? They had no land to farm, no cattle to herd. What they ate came from the people whose act of giving was in worship to God, who, in turn, ministered to their needs through the ministrations of the priests.

Although many circumstances have changed, it is important to keep these cornerstones in mind. When you answered a call to pastoral ministry, you said yes to a complete commitment to God's work in the world as a leader. You vowed to give yourself to order the worship of the people without attachments that would encumber that ministry and you promised to go anywhere and be without a particular place except among the people.

A few years ago, a close friend approached me with a killer idea. He knew that pastors and church leaders are not usually the best paid in the world. He also knew that my children would be headed to college in a few years and tuition was skyrocketing.

He had stumbled on a great plan that allowed for me to get involved in a side business that would multiply my money quickly and he proposed that I do it to create a nest egg for the kids in order to provide a hedge against rising college tuition. It was a good idea from a caring friend who was interested in my kids. He had the best intentions. Who could fault him? I thought long and hard about it, even though an inner niggle kept me cautious.

After a few days of thought and prayer, my wife and I finally put our fingers on the uneasiness in the back of our hearts. When I talked to my friend, I told him that when I answered a call to ministry and took my ordination vows, I promised to keep myself free from any encumbrance that would potentially distract me from fully giving myself to the work of God through the Church. I had to say no to anything that could draw away my energy or best effort from the call of God. I had to remain disentangled in order to be completely at God's disposal. Thankfully, my friend accepted my explanation and was deeply impacted to learn the depths of what it means to be called by God.

Answering a call to pastoral ministry is much more than a job. It is even more than a mission. It is all-consuming, complete availability and separation from anything that might undermine responsiveness to the nudge of God's Spirit. It is more than learning a trade or being consumed by a vision and committed to a mission—it means making life choices that make you completely available and free from self-determination.

The call to pastoral ministry is different than entering a profession or discovering a vocation. While it is true that any vocation may be a ministry, the pastoral call is not merely another vocation—it requires disconnection from networks and encumbrances that are not required of other vocations. This may not mean that a pastor never has a home or never has to work as a tentmaker for a living, but in a real sense, the dependent and transcendent nature of the pastor is much like the Levitical priesthood of old.

This encompassing pastoral identity is a must to find effectiveness in the ministry. Without a call—clear, distinct and unmistakable—the pastoral identity will either be lacking or shaped around an ill-conceived understanding of pastoring as a career.

Most folks agree that pastors hold a role in church life that can be highly stressful and laced with pressured moments. Rather than assume a victim role and encourage the people's sympathy, pastors should recognize that such circumstances are part of their calling. To allow pastoral ministry to be defined as a "stressful job" reduces it to a mere trade.

In reality, the pastorate is not merely a job with a lot of stress—it is more. There are lots of jobs with as much or more stress than pastoring. Don't play the victim and solicit the pity of people just because you have to deal with stress. If stress is your problem, perhaps the real issue is your call, or lack thereof. In the pressures of ministry, hard circumstances represent the reason God has called you: to be the hands and feet of Jesus to bring wholeness to people. These pressures serve not only to refine the call in you, but also to solidify that call with ever-deepening roots.

In a condition of ineffectiveness, you will either find your calling refined and strengthened with new wisdom to know how to be deployed, or you will discover it to be false or lacking and leave the pastoral ministry. Understanding the nature and depth of God's call is an important element to your effectiveness.

Calling vs. Deployment

To be sure, calling is not necessarily the same as deployment. Often those two become confused in a culture that is defined largely by position. I was once asked by a reporter if I was called to the position I was assuming. I said, "No. This is a deployment that allows me to fulfill my call. My calling is much deeper than this role." At first there was a puzzled reaction, but a few brief words explained the deep respect she had always had for those called by God—she had not clarified it in her own mind. Deployment is circumstantial and tied to a place. Calling transcends both.

In many circles, our terminology causes some confusion about the deep nature of God's call to pastor. Denominations with a particular polity, usually congregational, often describe the process of accepting a pastoral position as "accepting the call," and church boards discuss the next pastoral candidates in terms of finding the one to whom they will "extend a call." These are perfectly fine as long as they do not confuse the ecclesiastical processes with the spiritual calling by God. One is identity-based. The other is positional.

Perhaps it would be a helpful exercise to describe various levels of call. Many folks describe it differently, but there should be common threads that run through any careful description of the call to pastoral ministry. Charles Spurgeon's words may provide a clue to those common threads:

> A man who has really within him the inspiration of the Holy Ghost calling him to preach cannot help it. He must preach. As fire within his bones so will that influence be, until it blazes forth. Friends may check him, foes criticize him, despisers sneer at him, the man is indomitable he must preach if he has the call of heaven.[2]

Let's describe the concept of call on four levels. First, there is the level of call that is the broadest—the call to discipleship. This is a call that God gives to everyone, inviting anyone who will to follow Jesus in discipleship by faith. Not everyone responds, but the call is broad and clear.

Second, there is the call to servanthood. This is a very important dimension of calling. In it, God invites any who will answer to follow Christ on the downward path of formation. Think back to our discussion in the chapter on servant leadership—it means walking the walk of emptying and humbling oneself in service to the Lord. This is a hard calling that sifts out people who are not ready to pay the price required for self-surrender, yet it remains a call to everyone.

Third, there is a call to full and complete service to God and the work of God in the world through the Church. This is best described by the ideas we have discussed already—the full availability to the work of God and to serve and lead God's people in healthy, transforming ways. This requires a deep, transforming work in the heart.

Fourth is a kind of call that has begun to find its way into our conversations with great ease and regularity. It is a call to a particular place or position—perhaps a more accurate description would be "deployment."

It is not uncommon to hear a pastor say that he was "called to pastor this church." Well, maybe—but more often than not, God issues a calling to full and complete service, and allows great latitude to determine where that calling will be fulfilled. This is both good news and bad.

The bad news is that it means you may have to actually think and pray to develop a sense of fit, and wisdom to determine whether to take a position or not. I'm not suggesting that God abandons you and expects you to figure it out by yourself—the Holy Spirit will guide, nudge, quicken and, at times, foil plans for a particular place of ministry. But this guidance is not a calling—it is the natural dialogue and conversation that goes on between good friends when considering what may be the best way to be fulfilled in ministry.

This is not to say that God never calls someone to a place. Remember how the Spirit called Paul to Macedonia? On occasion God simply cuts through the haze and calls someone to a particular job, but be careful about basing a decision for deployment on God and saying that you are called to it. When it suddenly goes bad, does it mean you weren't really called? Don't blame on God what God wants you to assume in your own journey as a responsible, Spirit-led pastor.

The good news is that when you find yourself in a tough deployment and things are truly falling apart around you, your calling need not be undermined. Just because you are not effective where you are now doesn't mean you are not called by God to complete availability and dependence on the Spirit and the Church. Your calling may be intact and healthy, though your deployment may be a misfit.

Recently, I helped a large church through the process of a pastoral transition. It was painful for many and hurtful to the church, largely because of confusion on the pastor's part regarding the nature of God's call. For some reason, he was equating God's call with that particular position. Clinging tenaciously to the position, he created tension, division and hurt among people in the congregation who had for many years been good friends and partners in the church.

An ill-formed understanding of calling allowed the pastor to become the issue of divisiveness. Once you become the main issue in the church, your time is done. Fighting to retain your role does no one any good. In fact, it can easily become hurtful not just to the church but also to the view of the pastoral office in the minds of the people. Suddenly they begin to see it as a position to be defended, cherished and sought after, not understanding that a calling to pastoral ministry always transcends a particular position of deployment.

Tough deployments can serve to focus the nature of your call so that you can, with greater wisdom, be better deployed in ministry. Keep a healthy distinction between call and deployment. You may come to the conclusion that taking a particular church role seems wise to you and the Holy Spirit, and that will give outlet to your call. You may be like the 125-pound football player: Just because you don't do so well playing tackle doesn't mean you should give up football. Try tight end or running back, and maybe the passion that got you into the game to begin with will be rekindled and you will find effectiveness.

Clarifying the Call

So what happens if you are not effective in your pastoral ministry? Well, it may be a simple matter of deployment. Hopefully you have an overseer or peer pastors who can speak into your life with honest love to describe what they see and you cannot. Do not ignore those people, and when they bring hard words, do not react in defensiveness. Your ineffectiveness may be a simple matter that need not threaten your ego, much less your calling. If you are called, those kinds of moments may be difficult, but they need not be destructive. Your calling should give you freedom to explore those questions with honesty.

On the other hand, there may be real cases where your calling comes into question. This is a very sober season in your life. Do not shy away from it, but don't walk through it alone, either. Invariably, the human self will try to take control and defend itself when left to isolated contemplation. Find a spiritual director, an overseer, a respected peer pastor. Together with the pledge of honesty from your spouse, if you're married, embrace fully the doubt and walk the journey of investigation.

Here are four questions that may help you on that journey. It is so important that we could not leave this issue without some kind of handholds for you to grasp. Even if you are secure in your calling, clarity is so important to effectiveness that these may also serve to deepen your own. These are not the only questions that may elicit good, prayerful reflection, but we hope they will start your mind down the right path and give expression to your desire to walk the journey. Above all, walk this journey of investigation in the close company of the Holy Spirit and godly, wise friends.

Two of these four questions are subjective and deal with the internal nature of your call, while the other two are objective and deal with external factors.

1. Can I describe an encounter with God wherein I sensed clearly God's nudging or voice urging me to give myself completely to availability and dependence in creating health and growth in the Church?

2. Are there godly, wise others who affirm that I am called to lead and pastor in the Church?

3. Do I sense an inner fulfillment and peace when I am engaged in activities that fulfill my calling? Is there a clear intersection of my personality, passions and calling that results in dynamic synergy in my heart?

4. Are there observable outcomes that are recognized by me and other wise persons that build the Church and are consistent with my call?

The key elements in these questions are:

• The inner witness that you have in response to the Holy Spirit (be prayerfully available about this)

• The evidence of results or fruitfulness that comes from your ministry (be honest about this one)

• The affirmation of wise others (be receptive about this one)

* * *

Your calling may be your most precious gift from God, short of salvation. It is not intended to prop up faltering ministry. It is not intended to redefine failure as success in ministry. It is not intended to be reduced to a mere job or even a vocation. It is not intended to elicit sympathetic responses from laity for the tough circumstances that often accompany it.

Your call is a gift from God. Its value is not in the discharge of duties—its value derives from the One who has called you. Whether others value it or not is not important, though you strive to represent it well. What's important is whether God is pleased and the Church is deepened. Your call is a trust from God, confirmed by the Church, that shapes you. Hold that trust with great joy and thanksgiving, and take measures with God's help to clarify it for the effectiveness in ministry it will allow.

Notes

1. Os Guinness, *Rising to the Call* (Colorado Springs, CO: W Publishing Group, 2003).
2. Charles Spurgeon, quoted in Arnold A. Dallimore, *Spurgeon: A New Biography* (Edinburgh: Banner of Truth, 1987).

BIBLICAL FOUNDATIONS:

ACTS 6

Acts 6:1-5 is a mandatory stop on our tour of Scriptural foundations of pastoring. Amid a dispute involving the distribution of food, the apostles decided to select seven leaders to administrate the program. The rationale was that "it would not be right for us to neglect the ministry of the word of God in order to wait tables" (v. 2).

Admittedly, modern pastors may not view themselves as peers of the apostles. The model for effective spiritual leadership, however, is significant. When they committed to "give our attention to prayer and to the ministry of the word" (v. 4), the ministry of the Early Church prospered.

Effective pastors ensure the care of the needy in the church but do not allow physical and administrative concerns to become the primary focus of their work. The priority of prayer and communicating God's truth must be primary.

GODLY CHARACTER:

*Demonstrates godly character,
manifested through the fruit of the Spirit*

There are few things as good as a ripe, juicy plum plucked right off the tree. The plum tree in the Smiths' back yard was a beauty. Every year they watched the branches, waiting for the big plums to show up.

One year, the anticipated fruit didn't appear. The Smiths had no idea what had happened. A little investigation revealed the source of the problem: The roots had a disease. The disease was curable if caught in time—it wasn't. The Smiths' plum tree was still standing but it was fruitless. The painful discovery uncovered the fact that they were focused on the fruit instead of the roots. Good fruit always flows from healthy roots.

Darrel was a very gifted pastor—intelligent, theologically brilliant, witty, disciplined and great with people. Not surprisingly, his church was growing quickly. The denomination began to move him up in the ranks, and it was then that a few people close to Darrel began to recognize that he wasn't as patient as he used to be. He was often touchy and could lash out without warning. His doctor advised Darrel to lose 20 of those extra pounds. His wife was upset to find the *Sports Illustrated* "Swimsuit Edition" in his briefcase.

No one blew the whistle on Darrel because his church was expanding, his messages were powerful, his prayers were being answered in miraculous ways and the church budget was skyrocketing. But Darrel and those near him made a tragic mistake: They started enjoying the results and stopped focusing on the roots.

Darrel didn't crash, have an affair or run off with the church's money—at least not immediately. He just started sliding backward in attitude and approach. He pumped ministry up with the latest programs while his own passion for spiritual life withered away. The decline was gradual and not overt. When Darrel ended up in a hotel room with an elder's wife and church credit cards were overcharged with his personal purchases, everyone was shocked. Those close to him shouldn't have been.

Godly character is more valuable than good ministry skills. Both are important, but the lack of godly character has far greater consequences. Godly character without good ministry skills is a slow train headed in a good direction. Good ministry skills without godly character is a fast train headed for a washed-out bridge—people are going to get hurt.

Consistent, godly character demonstrated through the manifestation of the fruit of the Spirit is essential for effective pastoral ministry—priority must be placed on roots over results. Effective pastors prioritize the development of their character above the "success" of their church. They demonstrate the life of the Spirit through the characteristics that mark their daily attitudes and actions.

The apostle Peter identified this priority and underscored it in 2 Peter 1:5-9:

> For this very reason, make every effort to add to your faith goodness; and to goodness, knowledge; and to knowledge, self-control; and to self-control, perseverance; and to perseverance, godliness; and to godliness, brotherly kindness; and to brotherly kindness, love. For if you possess these qualities in increasing measure, they will keep you from being ineffective

and unproductive in your knowledge of our Lord Jesus Christ. But if anyone does not have them, he is nearsighted and blind, and has forgotten that he has been cleansed from his past sins.

Some pastors are nearsighted—they don't have an accurate view of where their character is taking them. If they live in denial long enough, they will become blind, denying their character flaws to themselves and to others. Just as roots grow around obstacles, these pastors build detours around their character problems so that they don't have to face them. They work around them, rather than removing them. Their priorities are to move their ministries ahead rather than to remove the boulders from their lives.

Focusing on the health and depth of the roots of godly character will keep you from becoming ineffective over the long haul of ministry. Peter essentially says, "If you neglect character development you will become ineffective and unproductive." Failure to focus on the roots of character formation will cause shallowness. A tree whose roots are shallow can easily be toppled, and neglecting the roots of your character leaves you open to being toppled by the forces of ministry activities.

Knowing the Shepherd

As a 26-year-old, I was heady and a bit smug as I stepped down from the pulpit. I had just delivered an enthusiastically received sermon to 2,000 people. As we began to sing the closing song, I heard the Spirit of the Lord speak very clearly: "Just a lamb."

I knew exactly what that meant: I should never be more than a lamb in the flock, always needing the Shepherd's leading, care and protection. If I thought my performance had positioned me for special privileges, I was deceived. How I followed the Spirit would always be more important than how I led people.

Character that runs deep with godliness will not only sustain a tall and broad ministry, it will keep you in a seeking mode. It will keep you soft, always seeking to know, to learn, to grow, to deepen. Deep roots of character will keep you a sheep. If you forget you are a sheep when you are trying to be a shepherd, you will position yourself for ministerial and personal failure. Follow the Chief Shepherd into paths of righteousness or you will be disqualified as an effective shepherd.

Character is the collection of inner qualities that determines your response, regardless of circumstances. Reputation is who people think you are, but character is who you and God know you are. Pastors who focus on character find that reputation will take care of itself. The word "character" comes from the Greek *kharakter*, which refers to an engraved mark. In biblical times, an engraver would make a repeated series of scratches in a specific pattern—this careful repetition resulted in an engraving. In the same way, character is formed through a repeated series of decisions. Each of those decisions scratches a groove in a person's inner life, and over time, others can predict how that person will respond to a given set of circumstances because there is a certain groove to his or her life.

Effective pastors are determined to build their character over the duration of their lives. They are on a quest to be transformed until they have the character of Christ. They long to erase the previous engravings of their pre-Christ life and be entirely engraved with Christlikeness.

The apostle Paul craved more of this character transformation even as he neared the end of his ministry. He resolutely declared in Philippians 3:10, "I want to know Christ and the power of his resurrection and the fellowship of sharing in his sufferings, becoming like him in his death." Paul wanted to experience the power of Christ's resurrection, but his focus was not only on the power that raised Jesus out of death but also on the power of the resurrected Christ operating in the believer's daily life. Because we have been raised with Christ (see Eph. 2:5-6) we are empowered to live a new life (see Rom. 6:4). "Becoming like him in his death" is an identification with Christ so deep that it can only be seen as a death to any other life. This union is lived out in a life of sanctification, a transformation that brings the believer's life into ever-increasing conformity to Christ. This transformation is empowered by the work of Christ in the heart of the believer.

Your pursuit of godly character is an invitation to Christ to engrave every aspect of your life with His presence—*this* is character transformation. The motive for the invitation, "That I may know Christ," resonates with the deepest longings of the pastor's heart.

One of my most powerful spiritual experiences was standing arm in arm with thousands of pastors as we sang these words: "Knowing you Jesus / there is no greater thing / You're my all, you're the best / you're my joy, my righteousness / and I love you, Lord."[1] This song, based on Philippians 3:10, captured the essence of what our hearts desired, and it's this priority on Christ that centers our pursuit of godly character.

Laboring for Inward Transformation

Godly character cannot be formed by self-effort. Non-Christians can develop *good* character through decision and determination, and while any advance toward virtuous character is commendable, those without Christ will be unable to develop godly character—that happens only through deepening intimacy with Christ. The heart must be transformed by the Spirit. As the heart is changed by the presence of Christ, there is a corresponding influence on the external dimensions of character.

Jesus was the only individual to ever wholly obey the commandments to fully love God and others, and His obedience to these two commands resulted in His godly character. The fruit of the Spirit naturally flowed from His singleness of heart. The wise pastor will give the same singular attention to loving God and others, thereby allowing Christ to produce godly character traits in her life.

Focusing on changing external behaviors can be counterproductive because transformation of character is a matter of the heart. Jesus rebuked those who were focused on the externals of character: "First clean the inside of the cup and dish, and then the outside also will be clean" (Matt. 23:26). Godly character does not ignore the outward dimensions of character; it simply does not start there. It begins with and majors in the heart. The integration of the Spirit of Christ with internal motives and external actions leads to godly character.

Solomon gave voice to this priority in Proverbs 4:23: "Above all else, guard your heart, for it affects everything you do" (*NLT*). Or, as the *New International Version* says, "Above all else, guard your heart, for it is the wellspring of life." Character starts at the roots of your life—it is drawn from the heart. The heart is the well that must be nurtured and protected.

There is a relentless enemy who hates godly hearts. Consider what happened to Isaac when he was being blessed by God: "So all the wells that his father's servants had dug in the time of his father Abraham, the Philistines stopped up, filling them with earth" (Gen. 26:15). Your spiritual enemy is out to dry up, fill up or stop up your heart so that life no longer flows from it, but few pastors are taught strategies for guarding their hearts.

Although godly character starts in the heart, it must move in a specific direction: It needs a detailed picture on which to focus. The mind needs images that the heart can cherish. Character will only ever be theoretical until it is defined in terms of daily living. Thankfully, God has provided this picture in the person of Jesus! Describing godly character is tantamount to describing Jesus. One of the most concise snapshots of the character of Christ is found in Galatians 5:22-23, which outlines the fruit of the Spirit: "But the fruit of the Spirit is love, joy, peace, patience, kindness, goodness, faithfulness, gentleness and self-control." This list of nine characteristics is a comprehensive foundation for evaluating the basics of godly character.

While the fruit of the Spirit and the gifts of the Spirit are related, the distinction must be kept crystal clear. The gifts of the Spirit are God-given tools intended to edify people and expand the work of God. In the iceberg analogy from chapter 4, spiritual gifts reside in the top of the iceberg.[2] The fruit of the Spirit, on the other hand, is in the bottom of the iceberg and must be the priority for the effective pastor. (Leaders who major in the gifts of the Spirit instead of the fruit of the Spirit are like many children at Christmas: They're so enamored with their newest toy that their focus becomes self-centered—they forget about the giver and anyone else in the room. Their attention to the gift may lead to disobeying Dad and Mom, yelling at their brother and ending up in a time-out for an attitude adjustment.)

As with so many spiritual realities, there is a both/and nature to godly character evidenced by fruit of the Spirit—it is not contradictory to talk about laboring *with* the work of the Spirit. Spiritual fruit is a work of God, but it requires action on our part. The clearest statement of this synergy comes from Paul in Colossians 1:29: "To this end I labor, struggling with all his energy, which so powerfully works in me." We give our effort to develop these character traits, but our pursuit is through the Spirit's power, not our own. The resulting godly character is not a product of our labor, but of God's work in us—yet without willful intention on our part, the effect will not follow. We raise the sails, God creates the wind. Raising the sails allows God to fill them, propelling us to be formed with Christlike character that manifests itself in nine primary ways:

Love

Effective pastors demonstrate a deepening well of love in their lives. Paul underlined this characteristic as the essential motivation for the life of ministry. Without it, we can do a lot of really right things for really wrong reasons. Without love, we are nothing (see 1 Cor. 13:2-3).

Each day must be a new lesson in learning how to love a God that we *cannot* see, a church member that we *can* see and a lost person that we *need to* see. You've probably heard the cynical cliché, "Ministry would be great if it wasn't for the people." This sentiment reveals the challenge of this kind of love. It's humorous because the priority of loving the people can be difficult, but loving people is far from a laughing matter: It is the core motivation for ministry because it is God's motivation.

Ministry is a love-intensive calling—if it is done well, it drains us daily. As a result, many pastors end up being love-starved. The only means to counteract this hunger is to create supply lines of love: learning to soak in the personal love of God, building a spousal relationship of love, developing friendships of love, and regulating the pace of emotional drain—all help to keep the levels of outgoing love high.

Joy

A professor once challenged me, "Live so your life demands an explanation." Effective pastors demonstrate an attractive spirit of joy that causes the world to wonder what their secret is. This joy resonates from a place that is grounded in the person of Christ rather than in the pleasure of circumstances.

A healthy child laughs frequently. He lives in a world of wonder and delight because simple things are splendid to his young heart. Effective pastors work hard to maintain a childlike gladness in the simple gifts God puts in their way.

Jesus said there was something wrong with children who do not dance when the flute is played (see Matt. 11:17). Some pastors get old in heart too quickly. God's flute is playing but they have lost their dancing shoes. Pastors who can dance with joy for a lifetime are almost always effective.

Recovering wonder, refusing to sweat the small stuff, rejoicing in small victories, reframing life to see your many blessings, readjusting your outlook for the future—these all deepen the well of joy. And if all those fail (as one person quipped), "He who learns to laugh at himself has an unending source of joy."

Peace

I love when the Pacific Islanders in our church greet and depart by saying "Aloha." They tell me that they are wishing me "peace, joy and love," and in this they have much in common with New Testament Christians— "Peace be with you" was the common greeting of the first-century Church.

Effective pastors bring "aloha" when they arrive, and leave "aloha" when they go. They are growing in the peace of God. Their hearts and minds are guarded by the peace of God (see Phil. 4:6-7) and they seek peace in their relationships with others.

Peace is living in the certainty of the Father's care and control. The psalmist was convinced of the two things he needed to know in order to be at peace even when the pressure was on: "One thing God has spoken, two things have I heard: that you, O God, are strong, and that you, O Lord, are loving" (Ps. 62:11-12). If God is truly strong and truly loving, then everything is going to be okay.

Peace produced by the Holy Spirit results in living at a pace regulated by God, operating at the speed of the Spirit. A word picture that can be helpful here is the oxen and yoke, which Jesus referred to in Matthew 11. In ministry, I pull alongside the Spirit. If I stay in step, then "his yoke is easy and his burden is light," but if I speed ahead or drag behind, the pressure of the yoke pulls roughly against my neck until I get back in step.

The Pacific Islanders at our church are on fire for God at a hang-loose pace. It is a "cool urgency" and it reminds me of the speed at which Jesus probably moved. I am impressed that Jesus never ran to get somewhere in a hurry. He never rented a chariot to accomplish more in one week. He knew there was enough time in one day to accomplish all that the Father wanted done, *if* he walked at the pace of the Spirit.

Patience

The Greek word for "patience" (*makrothumia*) can be translated "long heat," which is a great description of the person who is slow to heat up in anger. They have a long fuse.

Daniel Goleman points out that a person with low emotional intelligence is easily and quickly engulfed in the flood of his or her own emotions, but a person with high emotional intelligence is capable of refusing to react to his or her feelings.[3] Instead of flying off the handle, the person steps back and evaluates his or her emotions before taking action on them. While we must never forget that the fruit of the Spirit are a work of the Spirit, patience is one character trait in particular that pastors can "labor with" to develop.

Patience with surly board members, whiny sermon critics, rebellious staff, worship leaders with big egos and even discontented family members is required in ministry, and it takes Spirit-lengthened patience to avoid being engulfed in emotions that ignite explosions. As with many of the works of God in us, patience is another face of trust. It is not the result of forced or willful inaction—it is the confidence that God is involved and will, in time, shape the outcomes. Patience is practiced by those who don't have to have things their way and in their own time.

Kindness

One trait I look for when hiring church staff is how they treat children and the elderly. If they will kneel down to get at eye level with a child or with a great-grandmother in a wheelchair, they display a spiritual fruit of great value. It's an act of kindness to get on a different level than your own.

Kindness is being alert to the opportunities to contribute to the happiness, comfort or needs of another person. It is a sensitivity that watches for chances to serve in small ways.

I was out to eat recently with a visiting preacher who was absolutely rude to the waitress, at a restaurant that was a favorite with our church staff. I was too ashamed to pray for the food because I was afraid people would know we were Christians. People were looking at us and I knew they were evaluating everything they saw in light of that rude behavior. Kindness is a form of love and Paul tells us that "love is not rude" (1 Cor. 13:5). Pastors who are not polite are not kind. An effective pastor will embrace the scrutiny he is under and respond by being a model of kindness.

Pastors who consistently respond in kindness to their critics, their spouse, the poor, the weak, the young, the elderly and the non-Christian are pastors who manifest the Spirit of Christ.

Goodness

The call-and-response in our church is simple yet profound. I say, "God is good!" and the people say, "All the time!" Then just in case someone wasn't listening or didn't understand, I say, "All the time!" and the people say, "God is good!"

The spiritual fruit of goodness expresses what the Old Testament repeats numerous times: "God is good." God acts toward His creation only in ways that are filled with love, truth, nobility, wisdom and benefit. Since God is good, godly followers demonstrate that same goodness.

Spiritual people receive God's goodness gratefully and respond to God with praise for it—the fruit of goodness manifests a positive disposition and appreciation. They are "good-finders," seeing the good in people and situations. They have an approach to living that keeps them looking out for God's goodness.

Goodness loves that which is good or morally positive. Paul writes, "Hate what is evil, cling to what is good" (Rom. 12:90). One of the qualifications Paul gives for elders is that they "love what is good" (Titus 1:8). Pastors who lack goodness can enjoy badness without being bothered much. They can listen to entertainment or crude jokes or juicy gossip that should cause a Spirit-tuned conscience to shiver.

People may say, "Our pastor is good to everyone she meets," because goodness functions by seeking the best for those around you. Acts of goodwill flow from a Spirit-empowered pastor, and Paul encouraged such actions: "Therefore, as we have opportunity, let us do good to all people" (Gal. 6:10).

Faithfulness

The worship leaders at our church have never been late or missed a Sunday in 15 years of ministry, despite the fact that they gig until 2 A.M. at some of the top jazz spots in California. Storms, traffic, colds and earthquakes have failed to prevent their determination to be present and lead us in worship. They are spiritual people who display the character of faithfulness.

The Holy Spirit produces a steadfastness of character—the essence of a pastor who is reliable, trustworthy and persistent. The Hebrew word for "faithfulness" means *firmness*, something that is not easily moved. The circumstances do not easily sway a faithful pastor from keeping his commitments—his word is firm and his actions back up his promises.

A friend of mine used to be a wilderness guide for search and rescue missions, and he told me that 9 out of 10 times, the reason a person becomes lost is not because he is on the wrong trail—it's because he does not go far enough on the right trail. Paul was concerned that the Galatians were going to get lost hiking the trail to the harvest: "Let us not become weary in doing good, for at the proper time we will reap a harvest if we do not give up" (6:9). Faithfulness is endurance to continue in a good direction, refusing to give up, until a harvest is realized.

Faithfulness is also found in the cracks of our lives, the small places that we think are hidden, unimportant or unnoticed. Faithfulness is more than *not* having an affair—it's taking the trash out for our spouse, or really listening when our children talk to us. Faithfulness is built one small decision at a time, and unseen dedication positions us for greater blessings and responsibilities.

Effective pastors move past responses that are self-serving, quick and easy in order to look for what is best for others, even if it costs them. They choose obedience over expedience. They prioritize the principles they live by as more important than the products they are applauded for.

Gentleness

Isaiah and Matthew described Jesus' ministry as gentle: "A bruised reed he will not break, and a smoldering wick he will not snuff out, till he leads justice to victory" (Isa. 42:3; Matt. 12:20). Jesus did not callously use people to promote His mission—He gently dealt with their weaknesses. He nurtured the small light that their lives possessed, walking gently so as to preserve the faint ones around Him. He was known to shout at Pharisees and speak softly to prostitutes. Gentle does not mean soft—it means right response. When the heart is filled with Christ, it always seeks the right response, not one driven by emotion.

When Jesus rode into Jerusalem on a young donkey, He portrayed gentleness. In order to oppose those who lord their power over others, He chose a donkey for His mount. If you want to be gentle, don't come into a situation riding on the power of your office, high on your horse of personal pride or selfish agendas. Pastors should be donkey riders.

You don't have to shove people around to get what you want. When you evidence the fruit of gentleness, you don't push your agenda, promote yourself or attack people in order to get your way. This fruit is most easily seen in how pastors handle their adversaries and critics. Paul gave Pastor Timothy clear and balanced advice for dealing with antagonists: "Those who oppose him, he must gently instruct" (2 Tim. 2:25). Gentleness neither acquiesces nor attacks. It is appropriate tenderness mixed with truth.

Displaying gentleness in public is not usually as difficult as possessing it in private. How a pastor speaks with the staff, her spouse and her children is the truer test of this fruit because pastors may live in such frustration that those near them bear the brunt of their harshness when circumstances push them over the edge. When the character of God is working deeply, the evidence will naturally come in the form of a gentle disposition.

Self-Control

In a culture that majors on self-indulgence, self-control is a difficult trait to develop. At first glance, self-control seems like a negative, joy-killing, grit-your-teeth-and-just-do-it form of denial. Just say no to dessert, to that new driving iron, to the latest gizmo and just say yes to the exercise you don't feel like doing, the board member you don't feel like calling, the cleaning your spouse wants done.

Effective pastors understand that self-control is a means of denying a lower impulse in order to attain a higher good—sacrifice is giving up something that you want for something that you want even more. Self-control is a daily necessity for a pastor who is going to live up to his potential. He understands that discipline is not a choice; it is an inescapable reality.

During his term as president, Lyndon Johnson was somewhat overweight. One day his wife challenged him with this blunt assertion: "You can't run the country if you can't run yourself." Conceding Mrs. Johnson's observation, LBJ lost 23 pounds.

Self-control evinces a character that is being transformed by a different set of priorities. As that transformation occurs within your heart, you will begin to find that what you used to be drawn to gives way to new and different attractions. Yielding to the Spirit gives you the ability to walk away from old haunts toward new habits that are consistent with a godly character, whether it's walking past the dessert tray, avoiding the porn site or staying out of the Lay-Z-Boy with the remote.

It is interesting that when we are living Spirit-controlled lives, it produces self-control: Saying yes to the Spirit empowers you to say no to yourself. It is an irony of the kingdom of God that self-control comes from yielding control. Release to the Spirit returns power to say no, not only because the Spirit strengthens the will, but because the character within is transformed, and desires and priorities are rewired.

Effective pastors refuse to depend on their own willpower and instead ask the Spirit to empower the will. Strength comes from surrender. In that surrendered strength, Solomon's word picture takes on new meaning: "Like a city whose walls are broken down is a man who lacks self-control" (Prov. 25:28). Without walls, a city is defenseless and will be taken captive by the enemy, but strong walls protect the city so that those inside can prosper and those outside can be influenced by its resources. For the pastor with godly character, self-control is like the city with walls built, not by human hands, but by the work of God.

* * *

These nine traits of the fruit of the Spirit are the evidence of a character being formed in godliness, and the key to inner character transformation is a focus on the Holy Spirit. It is significant that God uses the singular "fruit" instead of the plural "fruits." These character traits are nine aspects of the fruit of the Spirit. My aim is not to work on love today, patience tomorrow, self-control on Friday—my singular pursuit is to be filled with the Holy Spirit each day, yielding myself more fully to the Spirit's power and walking more consistently in step with Christ—*then* I'll naturally reflect God through my attitudes and actions.

A godly life gives attention to the roots so that the effective results of ministry will be a natural, organic outflow of inner transformation. Deep and healthy roots produce the kind of tree that will bear fruit for a lifetime.

> The righteous will flourish like a palm tree, they will grow like a cedar of Lebanon; planted in the house of the LORD, they will flourish in the courts of our God. They will still bear fruit in old age, they will stay fresh and green, proclaiming, "The LORD is upright; he is my Rock, and there is no wickedness in him" (Ps. 92:12-15).

Notes
1. Graham Kendrick, "Knowing You (All I Once Held Dear)," ©1993 Make Way Music (ASCAP) (Admin. by Integrity Music, Inc.). All rights reserved. International copyright secured.
2. Kevin Mannoia, *The Integrity Factor* (Vancouver, BC: Regent College Publishing, 2006).
3. David Goleman, *Emotional Intelligence* (New York: Bantam Books, 1997).

John Wesley emphasized empowerment as a hallmark of effectiveness. In addition to *grace* and *fruit*, *gifts* were a primary focal point in the examinations that Methodist pastors underwent annually.

Gifts has two foci: natural endowments and acquired talents. Wesley was primarily interested in the natural mental faculties and the ability of a pastor to communicate. Can the pastor think logically and can he preach the Word in an engaging manner? In addition, Wesley believed an effective pastor should have a clear understanding of essential doctrines and be able to explain them clearly.

PERSONAL ACCOUNTABILITY:

Invites and embraces personal accountability

The landscape was barren and boring on I-10, a long, straight highway that cuts through the changeless west Texas landscape. The kids were asleep in the backseat and all I could do was let my mind wander. Even my hands and feet seemed useless. On such a straight highway, it felt like a waste to have to keep them on the wheel, stationary, unmoving—holding the car pointed in the same direction for what seemed forever.

As I gazed across the horizon, I noticed regular interruptions: what appeared to be tall toothpicks sticking up from the ground, faint against the sky. As we got closer to some of them, I realized they were tall, *very* tall, towers rising above the ground—perhaps only a few feet across, they were hundreds of feet tall. They were fuzzy on the horizon because they weren't solid spires but frameworks of metal.

On closer scrutiny, I noticed that they had virtually no foundation. Instead of broadening out at the bottom into a wider base, they actually narrowed further—the framework of each tower convened at a small, single point at the bottom. It was an amazing sight, and hard to imagine. How could something so tall and slight, reaching high into the sky and built on a tiny pinpoint of foundation, remain upright . . . especially in an East Texas wind? It defied good sense.

But as I looked closer, I saw the most important component of the towers: Virtually invisible until I got close, was a system of wires that surrounded each tower. Attached at various levels up and down the frame, the wires extended down and out in a broad pattern around the base.

Firmly rooted in the earth, they created a network of support for the otherwise fragile-looking tower as it reached the necessary height to broadcast the signals for which it was built. Each wire provided tension against the tower falling in any one direction. The tower remained straight in the face of all kinds of nature's forces because the system of wires held it vertical. If only a few of them were to fail, the tower would be vulnerable. Even though the tower had such a small foundation and was so tall, those wires were a system of accountability for the tower to do what would otherwise be impossible.

Mutuality

Effective pastors have close friends with whom they share life. They are friends who are quick to challenge or to affirm the pastor toward godly character and personal excellence.

> This is a person who has friends . . . intimate friends who share life with him or her on a regular basis. There is an air of respect, of mutuality between them. In this context, friends feel free to challenge the pastor in a positive way and cause him/her to aspire to higher quality of life. They are quick to listen and they are quick to affirm or rebuke as the moment calls. This, by the way, could be one of the areas where most pastors and Christian leaders fall short. We do not excel in either the teachability or humility that makes these relationships possible.[1]

The Kingdom principle of mutuality is an important principle for pastors who constantly face the forces of a culture and an enemy set on causing them to fall. The natural inclinations of the human heart coupled with the lure of an ungodly culture and the forces of the enemy create a hostile and formidable environment in which to grow tall and straight in pastoral effectiveness.

Alone, built on the small foundation of his own ability, a pastor stands virtually no chance of remaining undefeated. It is only when the pastor embraces the deep and mysterious work of being mutually submitted to one another that a network of accountability wires can be established to hold him straight and tall. The taller or higher he grows in ministry effectiveness, the stronger and more evident the system must be.

Mutuality requires that you acknowledge your own inadequacy to maintain equilibrium apart from others around you. It demands that you adopt a heart of vulnerability, which means that you open yourself to the stabilizing forces of other trusted ones in your life. Mutuality will not exist where vulnerability is not present.

It's important to note that vulnerability and transparency are different, especially in a relationship of accountability. When you are transparent, you show people something about yourself but you retain control of it and they can't really hurt you. Many pastors learn to preach with higher levels of transparency when they discover that people prefer it, but that transparency is more a means to communicate better than it is true access to their lives.

Vulnerability, on the other hand, is giving people access to you and also giving them control so that, if they choose, they can hurt you. It is not only divulging information, it is relinquishing control of it to someone else. True accountability requires vulnerability, not just transparency.

Vulnerability is something motivated by a deep desire to *know*—to know God, to know yourself and to know your people. You can only know them to the extent you are willing to be known.[2] Think about the pattern of Jesus in John 10. As the Good Shepherd, His deepest desire is that we know His voice and follow Him. To that end—so that we may know Him—Jesus voluntarily laid down His life for the sheep: us. God's desire to know us began with a willingness to be known. God voluntarily became one of us and continued the great act of vulnerability when He gave us the option—control—to reject Him. Which we did. But without that first step of vulnerability on God's part, we would have no ability to know God. It is because of God's choice for vulnerability that we have the possibility of knowing God.

Partners in mutuality must have deeper access than merely the top of the iceberg. A true network of accountability must be people who are allowed to see the pastor as an integrated person whose behaviors and performance are a natural outflow of identity and character. In this respect, accountability for pastors is not very different from the accountability in any disciple of Christ. The difference is that because they are higher-profile leaders and represent a call to holy living, their tower is taller and the network of accountability must be more deeply ensconced. This is the burden of leadership.

Knee to Knee

One of the most important factors in John Wesley's ministry was his emphasis on accountability for new believers to become "classic Christians." The Methodist movement was built not so much on the preaching of the Wesleys, but on the strong "method" of ordering life to transform minds, emotions and behavior in a sophisticated system of accountability called "classes." George Whitefield, an equally effective evangelist, once remarked that in comparing Wesley's ministry to his own, Whitefield's converts were like sand pouring through his hand. He saw the significant emphasis on life transformation in those who were converted by Wesley's ministry that only came through accountability.

Not long ago, my family and I visited the Wesley Chapel in London. The dean of the chapel graciously opened the museum for us to enjoy. Although there were many interesting lessons from history, one in particular stood out. In a replica of a Methodist meeting hall, we noted that the setup was familiar, with all the benches facing the pulpit. The preacher instructed the people in what we know as preaching. For Wesley, this was a significant learning time requiring deep thinking at the cognitive level. We're quite familiar with that, as most churches today are built around the pulpit.

But Wesley's genius was that he realized that truth is not truth until it is hammered out on the anvil of reality—and that requires transformation of the effects (feelings) and transformation of behavior (actions). Transformation that goes beyond the cognitive realm cannot be accomplished apart from a community in which there is accountability. Knowing this, Wesley had special benches built for his small-class meetings. Each of the benches in the meeting hall was built with a hinge at the base of the back support. At a certain point in the service, after hearing the preaching of the Word, people stood and tilted the back of every other bench in the opposite direction. Now, instead of multiple rows of benches all facing the pulpit in the front, the hall became sets of benches facing each other. The people reseated themselves knee to knee, facing one another, to ask questions about the condition of each others' souls.

In this fashion, cognitive learning was integrated into lives such that, on leaving, people applied the life-changing gospel in new behavioral patterns of daily living. They knew that in a few days they would once again be knee to knee with someone who not only was watching them live their life from day to day, but who would also be asking questions of accountability in Christian living.

Most denominations or groups of churches have built structures based on the need for accountability—the intent is to provide regular systems that help to get personal accountability into the lives of pastors and other leaders. It is easy for young, idealistic and entrepreneurial pastors to see these systems as "hoops to jump through," but they were put in place for a reason. Structural accountability depends on people, not the structures—it's only as good as the attitude you bring to it. (And, admittedly, it's only as good as the people who make the structure work. It's easy for structural accountability to become administrative in nature, dealing only with performance and top-of-the-iceberg issues. Where this occurs, it signals a misaligned emphasis on building the institution.) Don't dismiss the accountability structures of your group or denomination quickly. Bring to it a humble attitude of mutuality that recognizes your need for accountability. Be willing to sit knee to knee with your brothers and sisters in ministry and answer honest questions about your life and priorities.

If your denomination does not have a structure in place, make one! Every pastor must find some forum—formal or informal—wherein the principles of mutuality that result in accountability may flourish. It requires a safe environment and people who are trustworthy—because accountability and mutuality demand vulnerability, they are not something to be given easily to just anyone. Careful examination of the character of others will give you the confidence that you can trust them with your life—for in fact, that's exactly what you're doing. You are trusting them to keep you from falling.

Fortresses and Vitamins

Accountability has multiple purposes. The most obvious is preventative, but it can also serve remedial and developmental purposes as well.

We mostly think about the preventative function of accountability wherein the "wires" of other wise and trustworthy people keep us from falling under the pressure of leadership. Knowing that you will be meeting with someone who has permission to ask you hard questions and can see into your life can help to mitigate misbehavior. When you are on the verge of making a bad choice—doing something selfish, striking out at your spouse, watching the wrong movie, opening the door to a sexual opportunity—the faces of those intimate people pop into your mind. And for their sake, you stop. You say *no*. You put on the brakes. Those people in your life, with whom you have become vulnerable and have given access to your soul, hold you from falling. (Of course, you could manipulate them and falsely represent yourself, making them think you are fine while all along being duplicitous—accountability ultimately depends on your heart and attitude.)

Accountability is often a remediation for some failure that has already occurred. Perhaps you struggled with sin, but you were discovered early or you self-corrected in confessing it at an early stage. Good for you. Out of desire to keep it from progressing and gaining a stronger foothold in your life, you and those around you set up a remedial accountability system that is an attempt to "get the tower vertical again." Usually this involves intense focus and effort that is not sustainable over a long period of time. For example, you might meet with two pastors assigned by your overseer each week and phone each of them every day to report in to keep your heart clean. Or you might have people check your schedule each hour to know your whereabouts, or daily verify that you are not involved in any way with the money, or confirm that you have not lost your temper. It might be any number of formats, all of which are intended to ingrain in you new patterns of behavior that will ultimately become habitual. Layering behavior on behavior is another means to rewire your pattern so that your nature is changed. Remedial accountability helps you do that.

One of the most useful types of accountability is developmental. It's often not even considered as such, but accountability is not only important to guard you against failure or to remediate a problem, but also to find your own fullness.

Accountability that is only remedial or preventative is based on a fortress mentality. This is okay, but it tends to elevate negative behavior and create a basic motive that is fear-driven. The fear is that if you keep going down a certain path, it will lead to your demise as a pastor. Out of fear, you set up accountability to prevent or correct behavior. Don't misunderstand—that reaction is really important. Embrace that accountability and use it. But be careful that the basic fear that drives it does not capture your heart.

Building your life and ministry on a foundation of fear will not invite the fulfillment God intends—and most of the time, commitments that we make out of fear do not last long. Our human nature begins to rationalize it away in an effort to avoid fear, and pretty soon the motivation is gone and the preventive or remedial behavior stops. So, while fear may be a healthy motivation for setting up relationships of accountability for prevention and remediation, it should move beyond those and away from fear as the foundation.

Accountability that is developmental is like a vitamin—it encourages growth and leaning forward into what God desires for you. It is not motivated by the fear of what may result if correction is not imposed. Rather, it is motivated by a deep desire for *more*, the deep desire to be an effective servant of God in pastoral leadership. Remember, perfect love casts out fear—fear may motivate behaviors, but love sustains them.

Accountability that is remedial or preventative needs to give way to accountability that is developmental, and then it can become integral to your life as a leader. It will define your patterns, and the effect of its positive presence in your life will be a spirit of mutuality based on vulnerability. In turn, this mind-set will become contagious among your people so that the Kingdom principle of mutuality begins to characterize them and they become a healthy community of people weaving their lives together in Christ.

Seeing the Whole Shoe

A few years ago, I had a group of 20 undergraduate students in our living room. Once a month, they came over to enjoy life away from campus.

We'd play in the backyard or swim and then cookout and eat, following it all with an hour and a half of conversation.

During this particular conversation, I asked one of the guys if I could borrow his shoe. At first they laughed, but he complied because they knew I like to use impromptu object lessons with whatever is around. I tossed his shoe into the middle of the room and then asked three people around the room to tell me about the shoe, limiting their description to only what they could see.

The guy looking from the back of the shoe said it was an oval-shaped piece of leather with a flap that came down halfway in a semi-circle. It had a foundation of two-toned colored rubber with the letters N-I-K-E written just above it.

The girl looking from the front said it was a long object made up of various layers of rubber with cotton laces that weaved back and forth over the top. It slanted backward with a flap of tan rubber folding up over the bottom of the front edge.

The guy looking from the other side said it was a strange concave shape of leather that was short on the left side and taller on the right side, and the whole thing rested on two-toned rubber. The top was angled gradually up from one edge with laces hanging down, and it dipped in a bowl shape and came back up to a point at the opposite end.

I told them that from my perspective, it was a shape somewhat like the last guy had described, only it wasn't concave—it actually stuck out toward me a bit. There were laces hanging down, but there were no words, no crisscross laces, no rubber flaps coming up, and it had a big white rounded check mark in the middle.

We were each seeing something different about the shoe. What one person saw could not be seen by the other. Although this is an excellent illustration of diversity in the kingdom of God, it also points to the need to have accountable relationships with others whom you trust. They will give you perspectives that will help you fully understand the work of God that you're engaged in.

As I acknowledge that I'm not alone, I learn to trust others who see things differently from me. In that trust, I open myself to their input and influence so that my comprehension and the formation of my self takes on new shapes and dimensions that I could otherwise not see. Those wise, trusted others help me to become full—and I grow. But it all requires that I not only trust them, but also that I open myself to them. Ultimately, accountability depends on me and my willingness to participate with honesty and vulnerability.

Sources for Accountability

There are multiple sources for accountability. Each plays a different role and together they can be effective in your life as a leader.

Formal accountability is usually the kind that exists in the structural systems of your denomination or group of churches. Usually the ordination process or other systems of pastoral networking allow for formal accountability. Although it is often reduced to administrative functions and is easily avoided at a deep level, it is a source of accountability that can be helpful and you should embrace it as part of your ministry.

Informal accountability can be just as powerful, though not always acknowledged. Many folks just don't like the idea of codifying a relationship and making it so defined and functional, but accountability can exist in informal ways if you allow it. Your position as a pastor in itself is a form of accountability—your understanding of what that represents may be one of the strongest wires holding you up. Of course, this demands that you continuously invest yourself in understanding the nature and role of pastoral leadership (and it should not be something you rely on solely.)

The expectations of other people are also a very powerful source of accountability. This may include the people in your church, your leaders and certainly your spouse and children. Though others' expectations should not be your primary motivation, it is an important one nonetheless.

The source of accountability that is most often overlooked is voluntary. Because it takes work and intentional choices, voluntary relationships often fall prey to busy schedules or church activities, but it may be one of the most important sources of accountability *because it is voluntary*. In choosing to be in a small group of some kind, you must make time and room in your own thinking and be willing to know others so that you also can become known. Whether it's a small group of peer pastors or a few couples who get together for dinner each week, it happens completely by your choice and desire to have and give accountability. In that mutuality, you discover the power accountability has to hold you up and fulfill your own life and ministry in Christian community.

*   *   *

We will become shallow and one-dimensional without accountability, which will lead to ineffective ministry leadership and very possibly to loss of purpose or some kind of failure. In Kingdom work, we do not walk in isolation and we must not fall prey to the lure of independence. Everything around us pushes us to do things without help and glorifies independence, but we serve a different Master and operate in a different economy. Let us choose the fulfillment and effectiveness in leading God's people that can only come from the mutuality of accountability.

Notes

1. Gordon MacDonald, written comments on the *15 Characteristics of Effective Pastors*.
2. Parker Palmer discusses the dynamic process of knowing in his book *To Know as We Are Known* (New York: HarperSanFrancisco, 1993).

Few pastors consider their role without thinking about Moses and how he led the people of God through tough circumstances. Although his capacity to be effective in leadership began with his royal upbringing, the forging of Moses' soul and his identity as God's person is clearest in his experience at the burning bush.

When God called him from the heart of the flames, Moses felt inadequate and unprepared for what lay ahead. But God did not add any new equipment, skills or dispensation: He used what Moses already had, including his weakness as a speaker and his experience of 40 years of shepherding with a stick. When the ordinary gifts, failings and experiences Moses possessed were finally surrendered to God, they became extraordinary tools. The greatest work at the bush was not the rod becoming a snake, but the empowering of an obedient heart and a surrendered life. Effective pastors recognize that what they already have—when surrendered to the call of God—is useful for His purposes.

STRONG MARRIAGE:

Possesses a strong marriage with obvious loving regard for spouse

My wife was the first to speak as we pulled away from the curb of the parsonage. "That couple is going to have a hard time staying in ministry long." We had spent some time in the home of one of our pastoral couples who were relatively new to ministry. As usual, we tried to invest time to help stabilize and bless the pastoral couples in our care.

Mark and Brittany were recent seminary graduates and excited about ministry. Mark was full of the usual idealism that this was his destiny, that he could actually reach people with the gospel, that he could change the world for Christ. We celebrated their coming to the pastoral team.

Yet our time in their newly formed home caused both of us to harbor subtle doubts. My wife, who often senses the nuances more quickly than I, was troubled at the slight fissures in what publicly appeared to be a strong marriage and team.

"Did you notice how often she would undermine Mark with a backhanded attempt of humor at his expense? And the times when he sort of dismissed her as irrelevant?" Not exactly glaring red flags that signal a heinous sin—but enough to warrant some questions.

My wife particularly noted that it was pretty clear Brittany didn't support Mark's call to ministry—she saw it as a means to support the family financially. The fact that they were starting out at a small church with a small salary fueled cynicism in her.

My wife's intuition proved to be spot-on. Over time, Mark's and Brittany's habits began to spill over into the public arena. Comments found their way into public conversation, some made during church fellowship times, some remarks from the pulpit as a sermon illustration at the expense of Brittany's image:

"I couldn't go to men's retreat last month because I couldn't trust my wife to be alone with the credit card."

"You know, he never was a very good student. I had to do so much of his research for him."

These were innocuous remarks that were easily dismissed as a young couple "being real" for their people—or were they?

Within three years, Mark and Brittany were struggling openly with unmet expectations that they each had for the church. Hers were not met and the culprit was his lack of assertiveness. His were not met and the reason was her high demands on his time at home. They left pastoral ministry and are now managing a restaurant in another city.

The good news is that the marriage has not broken down. The bad news is that it was not sufficiently developed or healthy to sustain the kind of pressure that ministry in the manse brings. The marriage was not a fortifying influence on their ministry. Is this common? Yes. Is it avoidable? You bet.

Admittedly, not all pastors are married. It may be tempting for you, if you are single, to discard this characteristic as irrelevant to your case. Please do not do that. While you may be a single pastor and not particularly interested in understanding the import of a strong marriage on pastoral ministry, read on and engage with the underlying principles that are applicable to any intimate relationship you may have—perhaps with a close friend who walks with you on your journey of faith formation, or someone with whom you are building a close relationship that may be heading toward marriage. This characteristic is important to each of us—married or not—since our lives are never lived in isolation and the truths can be appropriated to some degree in any relationship from which we draw sustenance for our personal health.

First Stop for Kingdom Living

Effective pastors prioritize building a marriage that has a life apart from ministry, yet is fortifying to ministry. The pastor cherishes, affirms and represents his or her spouse equally in private and in public.

Marriage is the first institution created by God wherein the principles of the Kingdom are manifested. In these intimate relationships, Kingdom principles are the bedrock. Sometimes a marriage is a healthy, clear example of Kingdom principles reflective of Christian community and mutuality. At other times, these principles are not evident and the marriage becomes a contractual arrangement formed in the image of a contemporary, and largely secular, pattern of marriage that easily breaks down.

For a pastor, it is imperative that the principles of the Kingdom are clearly understood. After all, how can a person build something that he or she doesn't understand? You are called to be in the Kingdom-building business. If you ever hope to be effective, understanding the principles and the economy of God's kingdom is an essential.

Because marriage finds its source in God, not the civil authorities, and is the place where Kingdom principles should best be seen, an effective pastor must evidence a strong marriage—not as a prescriptive formula for ensuring good ministry, but as descriptive evidence that he understands the Kingdom and lives its principles in a healthy way at the most obvious and basic level.

Putting a priority on the health of your marriage translates into a healthy church. Obviously there are many other factors that affect the general health of the church, but without a healthy marriage it is almost a sure thing that health in the congregation will elude you. It is the sustaining structure that allows for the enduring of ministry stresses.

Often the marriage is the first place where the pressure of ministry is felt. Imagine for purposes of making the point that we conduct ourselves at multiple levels of relationships in ministry. At the basic level is our relationship with God. From that, we build a relationship with our spouse. Out of that abundance, we develop relationships with our children. From the confidence in our family, we minister in relationships with the people in our church.

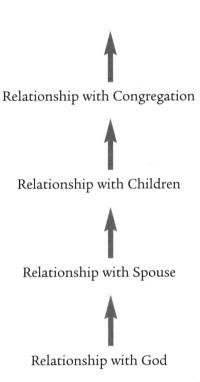

Relationship with Congregation

Relationship with Children

Relationship with Spouse

Relationship with God

Often, relational difficulties in the life of the pastor are evidence of trouble at a deeper level. It is not uncommon for unexplained relational difficulty to be traced to frustration, anxiety or pressure in the home. When relational breaches occur with children, it can usually be traced to an unaddressed crack in a relationship with a spouse. And, as you have doubtless seen, a struggling marriage is often the first place where a poorly developed relationship with God finds first expression.

Does all that mean that if you are having trouble in your church then you must have a bad marriage or that you don't have a healthy relationship with God? No, not necessarily. There are many factors that affect leadership effectiveness. But if there is not a healthy marriage that is strong, vibrant and growing, your ministry will, without a doubt, be hindered—if not destroyed.

A broken marriage is what Charles Ridley calls a "knockout factor" for those who are engaged in Christian ministry.[1] Billy Graham testifies to marriage's importance in describing his own relationship with his wife. He states that he and his wife, Ruth, study the same book of the Bible even when he or she is traveling. They talk on the phone almost daily and share with each other what they have learned from their Bible study. Bob Russell, of Southeast Christian Church, likewise makes clear the priority of marriage and family vis-à-vis ministry: "Do not neglect your family. Put your marriage before ministry."

The import of a strong marriage for those in pastoral ministry cannot be overstated. There are myriad books and resources designed specifically for this special dimension of the pastor's life. You may be reading this out of a felt need to find help for your faltering role as a pastor. It may be at this precise point that you are seeking some direction, so we offer some basic facts and handholds to orient you and at least get you started thinking about your marriage as a vital element of your ministry call.

Perhaps the most important factor to understand is that your marriage is not centered on your call or role as a pastor. It is separate, yet it has inextricable influence and effect on your office. Your marriage is first a gift of God's love to you and your spouse to give to one another—if and where it is built on the expectations of ministry or the activities of pastoring, a marriage is doomed to falter or fail.

Invest in your marriage separately from your church. No ministry is worth the breakdown of your marriage. If necessary, resign your church and leave pastoral ministry in order to build a strong and vibrant covenant with your spouse. For too long, the institutional church has exacted an "all or nothing" mentality that places couples and families on a guilt trip if everything—including marriage—is not on the altar of sacrifice for the sake of the ministry. Hear this clearly: *Your marriage comes before your ministry.*

The Love Triangle

A whole and healthy marriage is built around what might be called the Love Triangle. Not to be confused with the dysfunctional relationships you often see in the movies, this triangle proceeds from the scriptural call to love God with all your heart, mind and strength.

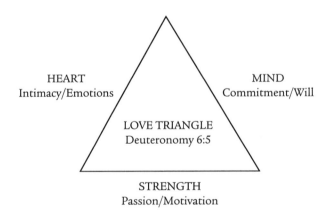

Your *heart* represents intimacy and the emotions that you give to another. If a loving marriage is a reflection of Kingdom principles, then the pattern of your love for God should be evident in your love for your spouse. In pastoral ministry, it is often easy to make your church your mistress or suitor. You may give to other people in your parish the emotional energy and focus that should be due only to your spouse. This is not what God intends, and it will lead not only to pastoral ineffectiveness but also to chronic marriage trouble.

Loving with your *mind* represents the reality that love is an act of the will that requires a commitment on your part—not just to establish love, but also to maintain and grow it. Taking your marriage for granted may be one of the most insidious threats to vibrancy among pastors. Love requires a daily choice to grow and strengthen it.

Strength brings into focus the motivation that is fueled by your passion. Often commingled with the visceral elements of our humanity, passion can easily become a rogue force if not harnessed and directed with careful investment. For a pastor who is regularly tied to others out of a passion for their souls and their well-being, the strength of passion can be held captive be the great needs of the community or congregation, or particular individuals who respond and reaffirm the pastor's investment.

Guard yourself to ensure that the love that is due to your spouse—intimacy, commitment and passion—is in fact directed to him or her and not misdirected or siphoned away by the demands of pastoral ministry.[2]

Marriage Myths

For pastors, a faltering marriage may represent a shame or embarrassment that is too strong to address with anyone. Perhaps you are struggling with this very matter and have kept it private for many years. Letting such factors go unaddressed will only make them worse and further undermine your calling—please do not fall prey to the myths about such a condition, such as:

1. *There is a back door for escape.* Contrary to the rising statistics across the nation and world, divorce or separation is not a solution that should loiter in the mind of those called to lead in the church. While there are scriptural grounds for such action, few of the 50 percent of broken marriages in the church today would qualify. The moment you give in to the myth that there is a back door for escape, failure is assured.

2. *Marriage is to make me happy.* While it is true that marriage can be a source of great happiness, it is not the core motivation for building one. The center of that myth is self, and building a relationship around selfish motivations is not a Kingdom pattern.

3. *My marriage should serve my ministry.* Subscribing to such a myth may sound noble, spiritual and sacrificial, but the premise is all wrong and the results will almost always be resentment, bitterness and failure of some kind. It will either cause a break in the marriage, loss of health in relation to children, or resentment in you, your spouse and/or your kids. This is not the equation that God intends for you. Your marriage is your first trust. Caring well for it sends the signal to God that you are worthy to be entrusted with a few Christ-followers who can look to you as their pastor.

4. *If I ignore difficulties, they will go away.* It hardly needs to be said that such a cavalier attitude will only breed infection, disease and destruction. This myth is equally true in your marriage

and in any leadership issue you confront in your congregation. If you ignore it, it will hurt you, the church and perhaps many innocent victims. It is an irresponsible doctor who ignores the symptoms of illness, presuming that they will eventually go away if left untreated. Likewise, it is an irresponsible pastor who falls prey to the myth that turning a blind eye or becoming distracted by the work of ministry will eventually cause the breach in her marriage to fix itself.

Facets of Marriage

Your marriage is like a diamond. When found, it is rough yet inherently valuable. Upon discovery, that diamond is placed in the hands of people who invest to make it sparkle, to give it worth that is precious, to make it a symbol of "foreverness." This is a process and it takes time and intentional effort. Slowly but intentionally, and often with some friction and grinding, the diamond is polished—one facet at a time. The outcome is a diamond with multiple facets that allow the light to be captured and refracted such that it flashes with the fire of wholeness and increases in value.

As you invest in your marriage, keep in mind the multiple facets that must be polished carefully but intentionally to bring the fire of purity and the complete potential of the gem that it is. Consider these different facets that when put together allow for the beauty to be seen.

1. *Marriage as a self-giving relationship with another person.* The principle of mutual submission is practiced and polished through daily intention and action. Mutual submission is not a means by which your own agenda is fulfilled. It is not even a means by which you achieve a deeper spirituality. Submission, by both husband and wife, is a natural outflow of deep love that

reflects the love of Christ for the Church. Such a love naturally submits itself. It pours out self and selfish agendas as an expression of love and upbuilding of the other.

2. *Roles within marriage can become a stumbling block as a pastor and spouse clash in their expectations of one another.* Whatever gender roles you choose—egalitarian or complementarian—they should reflect the principles of mutual submission. There are plenty of resources to explain the dynamics of these roles and to examine the theological foundations of each. Whether you approach marriage in a more traditional model where the man is the "head" (complementarian) or where both are equal (egalitarian) may be of little importance. In either case, clarity and commitment to mutual expectations is necessary.

3. *Permanence is the bedrock of willful commitment.* This is the source of security and the foundation of vulnerability. Where there is confidence in the permanence of marriage, a life of vulnerability becomes possible. Human nature would not allow deep vulnerability if there were any chance that the marriage were not permanent. If a husband or a wife thinks for one moment that divorce is an option, complete vulnerability will elude them. No one wants an "ex-spouse" running around carrying the deepest and most intimate knowledge of his or her soul! Without a commensurate commitment to protect and build each other up permanently, true intimacy cannot be nurtured.

4. *Communication is like radio: You can be transmitting, but if your message is not received, it hasn't happened.* The key to communication

is in what is heard, not what is said. When communication diminishes or ceases, the necessary vehicle for journeying together in a growing relationship is eliminated.

5. *Completeness is a both/and factor.* You are complete both as an individual and as a couple. On the one hand, you and your spouse are complete individuals crafted by God, yet the union between you should be complete. How can we understand this coming together of individuality and union? It is a mystery as great as the unity of diversity in the Trinity itself, but it is the life-giving source of your marriage.

6. *Declaration is an elusive facet that is easily overlooked.* At some point you and your spouse must live with the unequivocal declaration that you are one in this covenant. When you are first married, that declaration may require reminding yourself of it daily as you get used to the idea. In your exhilarating joy, it might even occasionally require that you pinch yourself to be sure it's not just a dream. Later, however, it becomes a quiet, yet pervasive, assumption in your personal makeup—the two of you are one in marriage. That daily declaration in words, deeds and deep conviction is an anchor that holds among the fluctuations of church leadership.

7. *Christ-centeredness.* It hardly should have to be said, but your marriage must be polished around the central facet of Christ, who is the third party in your covenant. This must be more than quick and trite lip service. In every respect, Jesus Christ at the center of your marriage will secure it on a foundation that will exude health, wholeness, goodness and love.

This diamond is valuable. It is not only worth saving, but it is also worth building and polishing. Neglect will not suffice. Taking it for granted will eventually lead to a fading luster and eventual breakup. Guard it, polish it and place it at the highest possible level of importance in your life. No ministry is worth the demise of a marriage or the breakup of a home. Even if you have to leave your ministry position to protect it, that is a far better option than protecting your ministry to the detriment of your marriage.

There will be plenty of opportunities to allow contaminants to get into your "polishing" efforts. There may be people in your congregation or community who try to lure you into an inappropriate relationship. There may be circumstances where you will be tested in keeping your intentions pure and single toward your spouse. Even your computer use may encroach upon the sanctity of your marriage. Guard against those threats.

Jenkins encourages building "hedges that protect" your marriage when it comes under assault.[3] If your computer causes a temptation, move it to a public place in the house or disconnect the Internet. If travel opens the doors to ensnarement, set rules for your meals, calls home and transportation plans. If your office creates too many opportunities for misunderstanding, remodel it. Build strong hedges that will keep out the snares of distraction and keep in the patterns of investing in the most valuable jewel you will ever be given—your marriage.

* * *

Remember, your marriage comes first. Without a doubt, as a pastor you will spend a great deal of time on pastoral issues. It may be that you actually spend more time doing the work of pastor than you do intentionally investing in your marriage—but quantity of time should never become a substitute for the priority of your heart. The person God has given you to walk with is a gift. Not only is he or she able to support and affirm you in your pastoral duties, but he or she can also guide and advise you in understanding your call. Mostly, though, by participation in the covenant both of you have made before God, your spouse will walk with you to find the wholeness, character and unity that God has invited you to in His kingdom.

Notes

1. Charles Ridley conducted research on the dimensions for successful church planters in his research at Fuller Seminary. Spousal Cooperation was in the top five that he determined were necessary for effectiveness to result. Without it, a person should not be deployed under any circumstances regardless of the strength of the other behavioral dimensions—hence the term "knockout factor" used to indicate that this dimension alone could disqualify someone for deployment.
2. Jerry Jenkins and John Perrodin, *Hedges: Loving Your Marriage Enough to Protect It* (Wheaton, IL: Crossway Books, 2005). Jenkins identifies the warning signs of misdirected love and to establish boundaries that will signal a need for attention and redirection.
3. Ibid.

John Wesley emphasized empowerment as a hallmark of effectiveness. Besides *grace* and *gifts*, an assessment of a pastor's *fruit* was part of the Methodist clergy's annual review process.

Fruit provides a practical measure of the first two categories, the observable result of grace and gifts. For Wesley, fruit was not measured primarily by numbers, but by impact. Has the pastor influenced anyone to receive God's forgiveness? Has the pastor helped individuals obtain a clear and lasting sense of the love of God? Has the pastor been an instrument of God's grace in the lives of others? In developing pastors, Wesley asked direct and pointed questions to assure effectiveness, indicative of the seriousness with which he approached the office.

Wesley adeptly balanced the priority on character and competence, on spirituality and practicality, on prayer and work, and on care and leadership. Wesley's emphasis on pastors who were both spiritual and skillful was a significant reason for the rapid spread of Methodism.

VISIONARY LEADERSHIP:

Possesses an ability to communicate a vision and motivate others toward it

I used to struggle with nearsightedness. I could see objects close to me just fine, but things in the distance were blurry. I could read with ease but I couldn't drive without the help of contacts. That was until the advent of laser surgery.

The laser surgery advertisement that caught my attention was "Two eyes for the price of one!" (That should have been my first clue: Don't go discount if you are shopping for new eyes.) I went through the surgery and was told to be patient for a couple of weeks because soon I would be seeing 20/20. Three weeks later I was seeing worse than ever. I couldn't read *and* I couldn't drive.

Then I read that the laser eye company was going bankrupt. I quickly went back demanding some help. They wouldn't refund my money but they offered to redo their work. That was a true dilemma. For better or worse I said, "Let's do it." Thankfully, the second procedure worked amazingly well. I now have 20/20 vision.

Some pastors see really well up close. They do really well in their near-sightedness—they can read and explain their theology books, counsel their people, create a great environment—but they can't see at a distance. When someone asks, they can't describe what they want to build. They have trouble rallying people in any certain direction. Their church calendars are a series of dots on the page that, when connected, draw nothing but confusion.

This kind of pastor finds it difficult to be effective. On one Sunday she may lay out a blueprint for a gospel ship, the next Sunday for a cathedral, the next for a hospital. There is nothing wrong with any of her ideas, but the lack of consistent, cohesive vision leaves listeners uncertain. The people in the church know they are supposed to hammer a nail, but they aren't sure why or for what. This type of church struggles to draw new seekers. They're like the Mexican-Chinese-Italian restaurant near my house: It's always empty. The place just isn't sure what it does best.

Effective pastors practice listening to God and collaborating with people to discover a vision for their church. They articulate this vision in public and personal settings in ways that influence people to help bring it into reality.

In the top 15 characteristics, there are only two characteristics that are significantly based on skill: preaching and vision-casting. Obviously, none of the characteristics should ever be totally dependent on skill, but because these two are so public in the church and are so action-oriented, they may be honed and developed as a skill to a greater degree than the others.

We have to be very careful with this one, though. In many respects, the desire for a healthy church is in itself a vision, and that makes it easy to slip into leadership principles that could apply equally to any organization, sacred or secular. Be careful not to equate visionary leadership with snazzy organizational principles that are little more than management expertise, because in the Church, this characteristic requires a delicate interweaving of the Holy Spirit molding the Body of Christ and the influence of a leader on the people and organization. Too much dependence upon the former yields a "holy huddle" syndrome. Too much of the latter results in a church that is no better than a franchise with a growing market share.

There are three essential components of visionary leadership: having a vision, communicating a vision and motivating to a vision. Having a vision involves being a ready recipient as well as the means by which the vision comes into focus. Communicating a vision deals with how the vision gets shared among the people. Motivating to a vision involves how the people are inspired in unity to move toward accomplishing the vision.

Having a Vision

A vision can be defined as *a clear picture of a preferred future that is worth building*. But this raises important questions. Where does that picture come from? Who describes that future? Who determines that it is preferable? What makes it worth building?

Pastors are generally viewed as vital to initiating vision for a church. Often those who describe pastoral leadership use a model in which the pastor is the point person for creating the vision. In this model, the pastor goes up the mountain with God and comes down with the vision for the church.

While a pastor-only approach to vision creation is not wrong, it may not be the best approach. It has its strengths, but it also has its weaknesses. While it may be relatively quick and provides singularity to the vision, the depth of ownership by the others in the church is limited.

Alternately, vision may flow from a group in the church, perhaps from collaborative work with the board, a task force or a congregational process. There may be a variety of ways that vision comes into existence. The important thing to remember is that *vision always begins with God* and it flows through leaders—lay and clergy—who are receptive and willing to handle it with care, as a trust.

Vision is not a sledge hammer intended to knock people into place. It is not a lever to force compliance, nor an advantage to gain the upper hand. (You and I have seen scores of pastors who treat it like that. The result is an unhealthy, often angry leader who crows about his success in people management.) Vision is delicate and essential. Without it, people dry up and lose heart. Vision must be quietly and consistently nurtured to become fully developed and magnetic in representing the heart of God for the people. It requires moments of soul-searching and struggle on the part of the pastor that may include a retreat to think, pray, fast and spend time in solitude with God. It also requires the pastor to open her grip on the vision and allow her leaders to have access, inviting collaboration and dialogue and a willingness to let them knead it as a means of shaping and owning it. God works through mutuality and interdependence to form the Spirit's mind among us.

If you are afraid of giving your people permission to handle your vision, you are holding it too tightly. If you refuse to accept wise and godly input to form vision, you are too insecure. If you trump people in your church by using your vision as a lever to manipulate, you are too self-centered. And honestly? It's not pleasing to God.

Someone once asked me what vision was and I gave an impromptu response: "It's what I see when I look out the window of our future. I don't create it; God does. But I see a section of God's mountain range. And I feel compelled to work with others to make that section reality." Working with others is an essential part of bringing the vision into focus. Admittedly, a pastor has to be able to see ahead to guide people to green pastures and healthy engagement with the mission, but in the economy of the Kingdom, it's not a solo performance. Remember, a pastor is a shepherd but a sheep first. If we forget that, we run the risk of arrogant manipulation.

A few years ago, I was working with a church that was in pastoral transition. On one particular Sunday morning, I was filling the pulpit and realized that these folks felt hopeless. They kept talking about how anxious they were to get a new pastor. Everything they did was in anticipation of a new leader. They kept saying that they needed vision—without a pastor they had none and as soon as a new pastor came, they'd be able to get going.

I took a few minutes before preaching to have a friendly, heart-to-heart chat. I told them, "I sure wouldn't want to be your new pastor!" That caught them off guard. "If you expect a new pastor to come and do it all, and if your ability to be a healthy church and move as God wants you to is dependent on a new pastor, then it's not a place a healthy pastor would want to be!" Now I had their attention. I went on to explain the role of a pastor with an illustration of a telescope.

Think about a telescope. Not the electronic or reflecting kind, but the type you buy at Sears for home use. It's a long tube, larger at one end than at the other. Inside that tube are a few lenses that refract, or bend, the light. You point the telescope at the moon and the lenses receive the light and bend it to bring it closer.

At the other end of the telescope is a small but essential piece. It's called the eye-piece. Have you ever looked through a telescope at the moon without the eye-piece? The light is very bright because the lenses are magnifying it properly, but the light is very blurry. You can't get it to focus. It's bright, but not focused. The lenses are doing the heavy lifting of magnifying the light, but without the eye-piece it's all a blur.

Conversely, have you ever looked at the moon through the eye-piece alone? You can see it. It's pretty sharp and fairly well-defined. It's just really, really small. The eye-piece doesn't magnify, it only gives focus, while the lenses magnify but don't focus well. Put the eye-piece back on the telescope and together the light is magnified and the image you see when you look through it is clear, crisp, defined and awe-inspiring.

As I continued with the congregation, I could see gears moving in their minds. "Your new pastor is like that eye-piece. Don't expect her or him to be more than God has called that person to, and don't abdicate your responsibility to be the people of God—the lenses. Through the gifts and talents God has given you, you must do the heavy lifting of magnifying ministry in the community. The pastor's role is to bring into clarity the awe-inspiring vision of God's scenery for a preferred future." For the first time, this little congregation began to understand their role in expanding God's vision for their church.

Pastors don't create the vision any more than they create the moon! God has already placed it before you—your task is to see the picture God has drawn and describe, by use of your talents and gifts, how your church fits into God's big picture. It will be filtered through your personality, priorities and experiences, but if you have made all those available to the shaping influence of the Holy Spirit, they will merely flavor the vision that proceeds from the heart of God.

God gives the vision, but it requires godly, competent leaders to point the telescope to the scene God has given. It involves using gifts, talents and collaboration to magnify that scene. Pastor, *you* bring it into focus. If you are disconnected from the people, you'll be ineffective. If you are pointed in the wrong direction, you'll fail.

Communicating a Vision

What good is seeing a vision if you can't communicate it to people? Vision is important, but vision-casting is equally important. Because you are the primary vision-caster in the church, it is incumbent on you to do it effectively.

Communicating vision comes more easily to some than others. Even if you have concluded that you are not a natural vision-caster, you are not absolved of responsibility to develop some skill at it. You may not be the best preacher in the world or a gifted teacher, but that doesn't mean you can stop preaching or teaching. It goes with the territory. It's part of your office.

Don't kid yourself and inflate your abilities beyond what is real, but don't give up, either. If you're not a good vision-caster, admit it.

Work hard at it and hone your skill. Don't just throw in the towel. Your people need vision—without it, they will perish! And they look to you for it. Get help. Use others around you—staff or lay leaders—who may be gifted at it. But always stay in the game. Vision is so tied to your office that if you give up totally, your effectiveness will nosedive.

Give your people some credit as well. You may not be the best vision-caster in the world, but they have the ability to sift through the things you do, the words you say and the way you conduct yourself to discern what section of God's mountain range you are headed for.

Although God doesn't give explicit instructions on method, there are a few clues in Scripture about communicating vision. Take, for example, the prophet Habakkuk. The *Amplified Bible* expresses it, "Write the vision and engrave it so plainly upon tablets that everyone who passes may [be able to] read [it easily and quickly] as he hastens by" (2:2). How is the vision to be communicated? Write it so plainly that it can be read and understood easily and quickly. As people hustle by they should be able to catch the vision. Billboards? Maybe. At least posters in the church, letters to your people, articles in the newsletter, phrases and words around the meeting rooms. Effective pastors take responsibility for communicating the vision clearly to the church and neighborhood.

THE MESSAGE paraphrases it like this: "Write it out in big block letters so that it can be read on the run." The *Contemporary English Version* says, "Write it clearly enough to be read at a glance." People live at break-neck speed. The faster they go, the bigger the block letters you'll need to use. That means that you make the vision readily available, not stuck away in committee minutes somewhere. It also means you make it in language they can understand clearly, not in theological or technical gobbledegook that requires an interpreter to understand.

The *New Living Bible* takes this direction: "Write my answer in large, clear letters on a tablet, so that a runner can read it and tell everyone else." The *New Century Version* says, "Write down the vision; write it clearly on clay tablets so whoever reads it can run to tell others." The vision motivates those who read it to run and spread the vision to others. You say, "But I'm not a good communicator. I can't speak well, or preach well, or write well." Who ever said that you had to major in speech or homiletics to cast vision? Moses felt the same way and even argued with God about it, but in the end, was there any question about what vision Moses and the people were pursuing? I don't think so. Use the gifts you have. See what you have in your hand, surrender it to God and let God transform it into the instrument by which you will lead the people.

Moses held a staff in his hand. It wasn't special—it was just a shepherd's stick. But he surrendered it to God, who transformed it—that stick became the tool of Moses' trade, and he wielded it to convey the vision and power of God. What's your stick? Maybe it's personal relationships, counseling, pastoral care, administration, preaching—whatever it is, you will be confronted with circumstances each day. You can choose to treat them as an annoyance and get them behind you as quickly as possible to get on with what you think is the real work, or you can see every one of those circumstances as a way to wield your stick and communicate more clearly the vision for the church. Everything you do is another opportunity to communicate vision. Don't waste any of it.

Motivating to a Vision

This part of visionary leadership is sometimes the most elusive. You may be clear about what the vision is and you may feel good about communicating it to the church, but unless the people are motivated to lunge together toward it, effectiveness is missing.

Most people are motivated *when they are involved*—that's a principle of leadership anywhere. Part of being involved means walking together on the journey toward the destination. It means linking arms and pulling together. You can't really be involved if you remain on the sidelines watching like a spectator. The healthy church is not a stadium full of spectators watching as high-paid professionals show their talent, and a pastor who treats the people like that is no healthier. The people will take their cue from you.

Effective pastors know the importance of getting people out of the pew and into the trenches. They bring talented individuals in their congregation to engage with the issues of fulfilling the vision. They harness the passion, the talent, the gifting and the energy that is in their congregation. By doing so, they develop deep ownership in the people for the common vision.

A greater motivation still is *understanding why*. Why are we doing this? What is the grand scheme? Seeing the big picture and understanding how we fit in helps us understand why what we are doing is so important. In the Kingdom work of the Church, we have the most compelling "why" a leader could ever want: to bring God's Kingdom near. To bring healing and salvation to broken lives. To reflect Christ well. What greater why could there be? God has given you the why of ministry. All you have to do is help your people see it.

When children are young, parents simply tell them what to do—do this, don't do that—and usually kids obey out of complete trust in the wisdom of their parents. As they grow older, however, obedience isn't quite so quick. Often they will do it, but not without first asking why. If you simply answer, "Because I said so," you have just undermined their process of growth and maturity, and you've missed an opportunity to gain their ownership in what motivates your actions.

I'm not saying that our people are like children, but we all grow and mature as we engage with the why of something. It gives us a bigger picture, a context, a connection that motivates us to join in the common vision. Invite your people into engaging with the why of vision. They will own it and be motivated toward fulfilling it.

Finally, *environment is important* in motivating people to a vision. Environment may not directly cause motivation, but a poor environment can foil the best efforts of otherwise effective leaders.

Palm trees are very sensitive to environment. They require just the right climate and surroundings. What do you think would happen if you took a palm tree and transplanted it to the Arctic Circle? It would die, and quickly. Why? Because the environment in the Arctic Circle is not conducive to growing palm trees (or any other trees for that matter).

Imagine that the vision of your church is a palm tree. In order for it to grow and flourish, the environment needs to be just right. Allowing the climate to vary too far away from optimum is a sure-fire way to kill vision in the church. You are the single most influential person in creating environment of your church. People will take on the qualities they see modeled in you. If you are an acerbic person, the congregation will soon become sour. If you are critical, they will become negative. If you are angry, they will become judgmental. If you are gracious, they will become kind. As you establish the climatic environment of your church, you make it possible—or not—for the vision to flourish. Remember the picture of the thermostat and the thermometer? You create environment; you don't simply respond to it.

If you create an empowering environment, people will feel empowered and take ownership and initiative in fulfilling vision. If you create a controlling environment, they will be hesitant to initiate, even though you feel as though you have control of everything. In God's scene of the Church, Christ-followers work together, each according to the gift he or she has been given, all for the edification of the Church. Empowering your people to a free but focused use of their gifts and efforts is consistent with what God has in mind for the Church.

It is precisely at this point that the other characteristics of effective pastors are so important. Because the vision to which effective pastors lead their people is part of the grand scene of God, it requires an environment that is godly in order to flourish. Trees have a natural habitat. Vision does, too. Godly vision requires a godly environment in which to grow and flourish.

Visionary leadership cannot be fully effective unless it is integrated with characteristics like personal integrity, holy living, prayer, Spirit empowerment and godly character. *Environment is affected more by who you are than by what you do.* If your life as a pastor is inconsistent with the characteristics of effectiveness that reflect the Holy Spirit, the environment of your church will not become conducive to a godly vision, no matter how hard you try.

* * *

One last idea is worth exploring. "Collaboration" may sound like a pop-management phrase, but in the Church, it is another word for mutuality and a variety of gifts working together toward a common vision. Because of the pastor's position, most folks defer to him or her to determine the amount of collaboration that will be allowed or encouraged. If you nudge collaboration into the fiber of your church, you will unleash energy, ownership and motivation in your people that will move them willingly toward the vision you bring into focus.

In a discussion with a peer leader about vision and my role in it, my attention turned to Barna's four leadership styles, not because they are the only ones, but because they help to capture the underlying principle of collaboration.[1] I knew that I was a *directing leader*, and I had also come to realize that I could not lead in isolation. Through years of leading, it had become apparent to me that I needed others with whom to join in collaboration for synergy and effectiveness.

As my friend explored my role in leadership, I told him that I needed the other three types nearby. A directing leader looks out the window and draws a picture of the vision: "That's where we are headed! Let's go." The *strategic leader* thinks carefully and naturally about the steps and strategies to get us there: "We'll have to travel along Highway 34 and then make a right at Highway 17, and finally merge onto Accomplishment Way." The *operational leader* naturally asks logistical questions and addresses the issue of what it will take to get us there: "We'll need 5 barrels of beans, 2 slabs of bacon, a Coleman lantern and 40 tanks of water." *The team-building leader* ensures that the relational wheels are well oiled: "Come on, let's get together on this."

You may use different terms or paradigms, but the point is that as you collaborate with others, you are far more effective in leading toward a vision. Furthermore, the results will be far more pleasing to God, who has made the Church a place where people need one another and work together to reach the vision He has given.

Note

1. George Barna developed four types of leaders as the basis for the "Christian Leader Profile," an online survey available at http://www.barna.org/FlexPage.aspx?Page=Resource&ResourceID=99 (accessed March 2007).

A FINAL WORD ON BEING AN EFFECTIVE PASTOR

You have been inundated with a lot of concepts in this book, and in conclusion, it only makes sense to offer a word that may help you keep things in perspective. If you're like most pastors, you either get really excited when you read something with which you resonate, or you are discouraged to the point of wanting to forget it all.

A lot of pastors go away from pastors' conferences more discouraged than encouraged—not because the events are bad, but because they feel so tired just thinking about what it will take to apply what they've learned, or because they realize how out of reach everything they just heard really is. Finishing this book may have a similar effect.

"How can I ever focus on all 15 of these characteristics?"

"How can I ever hope to really change?"

"Why do I want to give this book away and hide my head in the sand?"

"I can't wait to strengthen my ministry with the ideas I just read!"

Please be encouraged. The reason you feel extreme excitement or discouragement is because of the natural passion you have for your calling to be a pastor. When that passion comes face to face with something new, it either engages and grows or it fizzles in the face of a daunting challenge. The difference in response is largely a function of your inner condition. You may be tired; you may be at your wits' end.

If you are operating on the frayed edges of your emotional or spiritual capacity, you can easily become disillusioned.

You will respond to new ideas based on the condition of your life. Either way—in excitement or in discouragement—the key to assimilating the concepts herein is to understand a few things about your calling.

First, effective pastoring is a careful balance between activity and identity. Like the iceberg analogy, a careful balance has to exist between what you do day after day and who you are at the foundation of your identity. Once you allow that balance to tip one way or the other, your passion will drain. It's like a teeter-totter. One side is your daily routine of ministry activities, and the other side is the inner foundation of your being. Effectiveness in ministry comes when there is equilibrium on the teeter-totter.

The characteristics you have just read can help you find that balance. They should not become another pound of weight added to either side. They are not merely activities to pursue, nor are they merely conditions to become. They require careful integration into your life in a healthy, balanced way.

Second, these characteristics are descriptive. Beneath these characteristics is a growing, dynamic and healthy relationship with God. It is not the same as anyone else's—yours is unique because you are unique. Just as any relationship is distinctive, so too your relationship with God is like no other person's. Out of that vibrant and growing relationship, these characteristics flow naturally. By placing a priority on that relationship, these characteristics will begin to describe you in observable ways. Why? Because the One with whom you have an intimate relationship is having an impact on you.

Third, these characteristics are prescriptive. If effectiveness eludes you, it does not mean you are hopeless. Further, it does not mean you have a bad relationship with God. Focusing on building these characteristics in your life can serve to give the Holy Spirit access to shape and grow you. By focusing on these, God can do the work of forming you to reflect them well—as long as you recognize that they do not come from your own ability, but out of the vibrancy of Christ in you.

Images of Effective Pastors

I was 17 when I visited the museum at Christ of the Ozarks in Eureka Springs, Arkansas. After three decades, there is only one picture that I remember from that occasion—a large black-and-white image depicting Jesus as the Good Shepherd tending His sheep. As I looked closely, I discovered that the picture was actually composed of the New Testament. The *entire* New Testament had been arranged in such a manner that it created this compelling image of Christ. That picture frequently comes to mind when I think about what it means to be a pastor: a shepherd created by the Word of God.

Images we hold in our minds powerfully shape our lives and influence the ways we carry out our ministries. The office of pastor is envisioned in a variety of ways. Some see a bold Moses with the commandments under his arm. Others imagine a Nehemiah figure, guiding the construction of a church. Some picture a Barnabas who gently encourages the weak. Still others see a Paul, imparting deep theological truths with irrefutable logic.

There are seven primary images of the pastor. Usually these images are mostly subconscious. Rarely are they identified clearly and reflected upon deeply, but pastors need to understand the various images they employ in their leadership. Maximum effectiveness comes when a pastor realizes what images are most necessary in his or her current ministry context.

There is no single image that is synonymous with effectiveness. No pastor has the personality, gifts or skills to live out all seven of these images. Instead, pastors tend to operate chiefly out of one or two dominant images. As you become aware of yourself and your ministry context, you will understand what kind of leaders you need to bring around you to maximize the effectiveness of your church's ministry. It is by combining the strengths of several images that overall church health is realized.

Let's look briefly at these seven images. Try to identify the two or three that you resonate with—all of them are important and useful, but a few of them will fit you like a glove.

The Prophet

Pastor Joe is a gifted Bible teacher. He speaks the Word straight and no one would accuse him of being seeker-sensitive. You leave Sunday service well-informed. He's also not reticent to take on the latest sin of society. He's not warm and fuzzy, and people have left his church feeling uncared for. A certain kind of person finds Christ through his ministry, while others are frightened away. Joe's dominant image of pastoral ministry is the prophet.

John Calvin suggested that the traditional images of the pastor are prophet, priest and king. The prophetic image of the pastor relates to the proclamation role: The prophet received and communicated the word of God in an effort to move the people into the purposes of God. Although there is a connection, this should not be confused with the New Testament gift of prophecy (see Eph. 4:10).

The prophetic image of the pastor emphasizes the power of the pulpit to shape the people of God and to guide the church. The pastor views his or her priority as accurately knowing what God has said primarily through the Word, and then faithfully proclaiming that to God's people. This may also include hearing what God is currently speaking in supernatural ways. In both cases, the emphasis is on presenting truth in a manner that moves the church to action.

This prophetic image is not limited to pulpit ministry. Pastors can have a prophetic voice to speak God's word in society in an effort to bring truth and justice. It may be confronting city hall about the strip clubs or networking with city business leaders to develop moral responsibility to the poor. Perhaps a prophetic image manifests itself when a pastor rides along with the city police to share Christ or knocks on doors to share the gospel.

Elijah was a great example of this image. He proclaimed in a way that stirred Israel for God. He confronted the sins of God's people and society. Twelve times in Scripture we are told that "the word of the Lord came to Elijah." Elijah was not out to win friends and influence people—his call was to speak God's word and say it straight.

The Priest

Sam is a pastor in the Midwest, and if one of her people is in the hospital, she's there with her anointing oil. If someone has a child, she's first on the scene, ready to pray the baby into the new world. At Sunday services, her favorite time is when she breaks the bread and offers the cup of the Eucharist to her congregation. Sam designates two mornings each week for people to confess their sin and receive prayer. Her church respects the seriousness with which Sam carries out her pastoral office, and they sense God's presence in their midst during services.

The priest image stresses the pastor's role as the worship leader who carries out sacramental functions on behalf of the church. Similar to the priestly role in the Old Testament, the pastor facilitates individual and corporate worship. The pastor administers communion, performs baptisms, officiates at weddings, leads the funerals, receives confession, counsels the sinner, seeks to reconcile relationships, and intercedes with God on behalf of the people. This pastor places high value on her role as a representative of God.

These pastors fulfill the role of priest as mediators, bringing God to people and people to God. Effectiveness is evaluated by an indefinable sense of God's presence being active in the midst of the sacraments and rites. Preserving the integrity, continuity and sanctity of the expressions of faith is the priority for these pastors.

Aaron's priestly ministry brought people into the presence of God as he offered sacrifices on their behalf. He spoke God's Word, interceded for the people, ensured the holiness of the temple and priesthood, and communicated God's forgiveness.

This priestly image, which for centuries was predominant in Christianity, was somewhat marginalized in evangelical circles during the last century. However, in recent years, there has been a resurgence of this image. With an increased use of liturgy and an emphasis on ancient-future expressions of church, this image is finding broader interest and impact.

The King

Pastor John is at his best when he is setting up the new budget for the ministry year or laying out the system for newcomer follow-up. He is excited by recruiting people for the discipleship program, training them, and then overseeing their work. Details are important to him and the details usually need to be done his way. He delegates easily, though he is often frustrated by the follow-through of those he empowers. His goal is that the church be a well-oiled machine that is moving in harmony with his spiritual leadership. Administration is one of his top spiritual gifts.

The kingly image suggests the managerial functions of the church. First Timothy 5:17 refers to this image of pastors when it states, "let the elders who rule well be counted worthy of double honor."

This dimension of pastoring focuses on leadership and organization. The pastor who embodies this image arranges people and systems in order to serve the mission of the Kingdom. He gives marching orders. He understands short-term and long-range goals and he develops and executes a plan for achieving them.

Moses was a multi-dimensional leader, but the kingly image describes a significant part of his leadership. He organized slaves into a well-functioning community. By setting up systems for worship, hygiene, law and order, he administrated the needs of the people. He appointed leaders who oversaw groups of thousands, hundreds, fifties and tens for the sake of dispensing justice and maintaining order (see Exod. 18).

Ministry would be chaotic without appropriate administration and leadership. The kingly role brings order out of chaos and sets the church on a clear path toward worthy goals. It sets boundaries and creates standards for excellence. To be overzealous in this image can, of course, lead to detrimental side effects—overbearing, independent, rigid or overly task-focused pastors will damage their effectiveness and, without moderation, can quickly take on the reputation of being empire-builders.

The Servant

Not long after I began pastoring, we took a team to the Dominican Republic to work on a church construction project. During the day, I sweated away with a pick axe, digging through what had once been a dump site for the locals. At night, I preached. I thought I was preaching pretty well, but I discovered that my actions were having more impact than my words. One Dominican summarized the group's feelings: "I will listen to you because your hands are dirty."

The servant image draws heavily on the example of Jesus as the role model for pastoral ministry. Robert Dale writes, "Servanthood is the basic image of the person and work of Christ. For example, when the hymn fragment containing the loftiest Christology in the New Testament describes Jesus, what term does it use? Servant."[1]

The pastor whose primary inclination is that of servant is "responding to the call of another, serving the poor and needy, participating with Christ in a self-emptying process, obeying as a slave to their master, and engaging in the call to self-sacrifice."[2] The servant pastor seeks to lay down his or her life for the needs of the people. This pastor finds satisfaction in taking a hot meal to a shut-in, visiting the sick, helping a member build a fence, setting up a blood drive for the community, cleaning the sanctuary bathrooms, showing up at the workplaces of his members, or mowing his neighbor's yard. His ministry is incarnational as he lives out the gospel in his daily activities. He carries out a *ministry of presence*, bringing Christ where the people are.

Incarnational servant ministry is on the rise in the church. The image of "being" the gospel to gain credibility to "speak" the gospel is gaining momentum. The world is getting tired of pastors who love to talk and then retreat into their wood-lined studies until next week's speech. There is little authority in hands that hit the computer keys but never serve the needy. Credibility flows from hands that are willing to be soiled by the needs of others. The message of life is carried in a life that is living out the message through service.

As with each of the images, there is a potential downside to that of servant if it is carried to extremes or not balanced with some of the other images. It can become a disempowering image in which the pastor abdicates leadership, causing the pastor to become a servant of the people rather than a servant of God.

The Servant Leader

Unlike the other images, the title of this image is not found in Scripture. The image of servant leader has been critiqued as promoting ego, individualism, self-reliance, competition and a gap between clergy and laity—but a healthy pursuit of servant leadership would lead away from such pitfalls. It is similar to coaching, which is a vocation of helping others achieve their potential. Coaching can also be an activity centered in ego, competition and pride, and can create division between the coach and players. The difference is that a true servant leader is a servant first.[3]

Paul was neither afraid to do the dirty work of serving nor to assert his authority to lead. He viewed tent-making, reasoning with philosophers, tending to the sick, gathering firewood, preaching to crowds, sharing Christ with political leaders and refuting heretics each as a response to following Christ in every circumstance. He counted leading, teaching, writing and reasoning as forms of serving, but his serving was also lived out in matters like helping the poor and sick.

As a servant leader, Paul was a spiritual entrepreneur: He was constantly looking for the next new opportunity for the sake of the gospel. He was relentless in creatively changing the method of delivering the message to match the audience he was addressing. He met new prospects with innovative ideas, and those ideas were always driven by his deep commitment to be a servant of Christ. He always sought to raise and empower leaders and to help them become more of what they were called to do.

These are marks of the servant leader. This pastor holds serving and leading in a dynamic balance. There are times to be in the trenches with the people, times to be at the front leading the charge, times to be in solitude creating battle plans.

The pastor who prioritizes the servant leader image will major in visionary leadership that is aggressive without being overbearing. Her goal is to fulfill the vision God has for the people while believing that God has placed her in her position to lead the people to that place. She steps into the authority of her position with compassion and with confidence in serving God.

The Friend

Brad grew up in a large church with a star pastor who could do it all. His pastor had an air of authority and a commanding presence. Brad watched as people were utilized to carry out the pastor's ministry objectives and then seemingly tossed aside. Sensing his own call to ministry,

Brad stiffened at the picture of trying to become like his domineering pastor, knowing that he was much more relational and not nearly as goal-driven. Struggling with this image led Brad down a different path in ministry: Discovering a network of house churches, he became a house-church pastor. Knowing each person in his church intimately and working with them to transform a three-block square of their community stirs Brad's passion.

Edward Zaragoza promotes the friend image of the pastor, drawing on a foundation of the friendship within the Trinity: "Neither servanthood nor servant leadership allows for friendship, because friendship is fundamentally relational and only secondarily functional. Nevertheless, Jesus tells us that we are no longer servants or servant leaders. We are friends" (John 15:15).[4] Zaragoza asserts that "Friendship is Jesus' paradigm for ordained ministry for us because it is Trinitarian."[5]

Friend is one of the most potent images for people. We all desire to have friends and to know that God is our Friend. The friend image calls on the pastor to act as a friend of God, a friend of people and a friend of self. This pastor prioritizes conducting her ministry as a partnership. She doesn't do ministry *for* the people but *with* the people. Neither leadership nor servanthood is stressed. The clergy/laity distinction is negligible.

The friend pastor is a ready listener, a consensus builder and a caregiver. The emphasis on task is generally low and the priority on individuals very high. Her measure of success and effectiveness is the depth of relationship she has with the individuals in her congregation.

Barnabas reflected aspects of this image. He was unconcerned with Paul's past reputation or potential threat to the church, focusing instead on welcoming Paul as a person, inviting him into the circle of fellowship. As his name suggests, Barnabas was a "son of encouragement," inspiring Paul to use his gifts for the building of the Church. Barnabas was happy to minister alongside Paul and see Paul's development as an apostle. The spotlight was unnecessary for Barnabas.

A lot of people, even seminary professors, question whether a pastor should have close friends within the congregation. This image would suggest that most, if not all, of the congregation should be close friends. It is as you live in authentic, close, vulnerable friendships that life change can happen most effectively.

The Shepherd

Shepherd is the most-used image to depict the multifaceted role of pastor, and shows up more than 500 times in Scripture. The relationship between the shepherd and the flock describes and illustrates what God expects of those whom He places in roles of church leadership.

Pastoral theology in the eighteenth and nineteenth centuries spoke of *poimenics*, the study of shepherding (from the Greek word for shepherd, *poimen*, a verb form that means to feed or to tend the flock). Through the twentieth century, perhaps due to the decline of the agricultural era, this term decreased in use, but Derek Tidball describes the necessity of the shepherding image in the development of pastoral theology in unequivocal terms:

> Pastoral theology, then, properly relates to the interface between theology and Christian doctrine on the one hand, and pastoral experience and care on the other. As such it is found to be a discipline in tension. It is not theology in the abstract, but theology seen from the shepherding perspective. The shepherding perspective may well inform and question the theology but more fundamentally the theology will inform and question the work of the shepherd and that relationship must not be reversed. This will give the pastoral dimension of the life of the church a secure starting point and will prevent it from going off at all sorts of tangents.[6]

The prophets, priests and kings of Israel, especially Moses and David, were called to shepherd God's people. Jesus' key description of His relationship to His people was one of shepherd. The apostolic charge delivered to Peter, perhaps as representative of all the apostles, was to feed and care for Jesus' sheep (see John 21:15-19). The duty of the pastor was summed up in Acts 20:28: "Keep watch over yourselves and all the flock of which the Holy Spirit has made you overseers. Be shepherds of the church of God, which he bought with his own blood."

This image integrates several of the other images into it. The primary elements of this image stress themes such as:

1. Relationship—knowing your sheep by name
2. Protection—laying down your life for your sheep
3. Nurture—supplying your sheep food and water
4. Restoration—searching for and rescuing the lost sheep
5. Healing or Counseling—tending to the wounds of your sheep
6. Leadership—guiding your sheep in productive paths

David was a shepherd boy who became a shepherd-king. He led the people in worship as he danced before the ark. Just as he had defeated the wolves and lions, he led in spiritual warfare against the Philistines. He provided feasts for his people. He found the hurting, such as Mephibosheth, and helped bring provision and healing to them. David led in collecting resources for building the Temple—the first church-building campaign. The psalms show his love for the study and teaching of God's word. David was also an organizer who established policies that served the nation well. That may have been partly what caused God to declare David "a man after his own heart."

* * *

As you consider these images and characteristics as tools for your ongoing ministry, involve others in making them integral to your life. First, take them to your prayer closet and allow God to seal to your heart the exact points that are yours to own. Second, reflect on them over time—rash and impulsive commitments are often broken when the reality of life and ministry hits. Third, invite your spouse or close friend into a healthy and ongoing conversation about them in your life. Fourth, trust the insight of those also in leadership—give them access and accept their wisdom. Fifth, take small steps that will allow incremental change and results to be noticeable. By that you will be encouraged and able to fine-tune your commitment and focus.

It is our hope that these words have affirmed and inspired you in your calling to be a pastor and have provided guidance to help you take a step toward greater effectiveness for the sake of the Church.

The Church is moving into a new day. Pastors are needed who are competent and godly—in other words, pastors who are effective. In a spirit of prayer and with a humble heart, embrace afresh the call of God to pastor. To that end, we work and pray.

May God bless you!

Notes
1. Robert D. Dale, *Pastoral Leadership* (Nashville, TN: Abingdon, 1986), p. 29.
2. Edward C. Zaragoza, *No Longer Servants, But Friends—A Theology of Ordained Ministry* (Nashville, TN: Abingdon, 1999), pp. 23-26.
3. Robert Greenleaf, *Servant Leadership* (Mahwah, NJ: Paulist Press, 1977).
4. Zaragoza, p. 70.
5. Ibid., p. 80.
6. Derek Tidball, *The Message of the Cross: Wisdom Unsearchable, Love Indestructible* (Downers Grove, IL: InterVarsity Press, 2001), p. 24

USING *15 CHARACTERISTICS OF EFFECTIVE PASTORS*

We believe and pray that this resource will meet the needs of pastors in a variety of situations. Here are a few areas in which we think the material we present in this book will be especially helpful.

Pastoral Self-Evaluation

One of the most important qualities of a leader is self-awareness. If you are a pastor or leader of a local church, these 15 Characteristics can be a starting point for ongoing assessment of your personal effectiveness. As you immerse yourself in understanding them, the Holy Spirit may begin to show you areas in which you are well focused, as well as areas that need strengthening. Be honest with yourself about these, because ignoring them can only have harmful consequences for you *and* your church.

You may be relatively new to pastoral ministry. The 15 Characteristics can help you to establish the qualities that will guide and serve you well over a lifetime of effective ministry. Perhaps you are midway through your life, wondering if what you have done is important. You may be looking for some mid-course correction or a checkpoint as you move into the second half of your ministry life. If you despair as you replay the last 15 or 20 years, find hope in God and step onto a new path for the next 20 with humility. Take time to deeply consider these characteristics, and remember that with God every day is new.

Maybe you are looking back over your life as a pastor. We hope this book will serve as an affirmation of the principles that have guided you over many years. And, just maybe, the 15 Characteristics will provide a vocabulary and a framework by which you can mentor and encourage younger ones around you as they begin the path you have walked.

Pastoral Screening

Identification and screening of pastoral staff happen at multiple levels. In independent churches, they happen on a small scale, usually by the senior pastor or senior staff. In denominations, they happen on a national or even global scale and are commonly directed by judicatory leaders or committees.

The basis of screening those called to pastoral ministry is often left to the subjective judgment of those responsible for the process. We trust the Holy Spirit to use leaders to beget leaders, but it sure is nice when we have some guidelines to focus our discernment! The 15 Characteristics can be helpful to boards, committees, superintendents, bishops and other institutional leaders who are charged with discerning who should be encouraged into pastoral ministry. Most of these characteristics do not require a pastoral deployment in order to be observed, so judicatories that are in the process of screening new candidates may greatly benefit by using them as a guide.

Pastoral Searches

There's not a church in existence that has not or will not go through a time of pastoral transition—unless the church dies when the founding pastor leaves! The process of searching for a new pastor is often tedious and occasionally divisive. "We should write out our expectations for our new pastor" is usually one of the first suggestions of the pastoral search committee. The result is invariably a litany of expectations that few could fulfill.

Can you imagine a pastoral search committee convening for the first time in prayer, reflection and dialogue about the 15 Characteristics of effective pastors, which have been offered by a group of thoughtful and qualified experts? It might become an exercise in unity! Our prayer is that it would become a process by which church boards and search committees deepen their understanding of the office of pastor, and through which church members can focus on God's vision for the local church.

One of the greatest difficulties facing search committees is understanding the nature of the pastoral call. Frequently, the profile for a new pastor gets reduced to a job description patterned after the local CEO's, with a few spiritual duties tossed in on the side—but the call to shepherd God's people is different to its very core! Who will help these well-intentioned people begin at the right place and grow in their understanding? We believe that the consensual wisdom of a body of pastoral experts is a good place to start.

Pastoral Training

Many seminaries and Bible schools approach education with an inductive methodology. First, pastoral ministry is divided into various components—such as theology, biblical studies, or counseling—and then each of those disciplines is taught by an expert in that particular field. It's not hard to see that success in pastoral training can quickly become about learning individual components and excelling in the classroom instead of becoming a whole, effective pastor.

A better—and broader—approach is to learn from those who are living it. We are not suggesting that the classic disciplines of theological training be replaced, but rather that they must be enhanced by an over-arching understanding of pastoral effectiveness. This will help those who are in training schools to see how their education contributes to their formation into healthy, whole, equipped and effective pastors.

THE DELPHI PROCESS

The process used to develop the 15 characteristics of effective pastors involved what is called a Delphi Panel. This is a long-established research method by which consensus is built among experts to determine validity. In other words, the 15 characteristics have been validated by our panel of experts through the Delphi Process. Much that is contained in each of the chapters is our commentary, but the characteristics themselves are validated by the panel.

> The objective of most Delphi applications is the reliable and creative exploration of ideas or the production of suitable information for decision making. The Delphi Method is based on a structured process for collecting and distilling knowledge from a group of experts by means of a series of questionnaires interspersed with controlled opinion feedback (Adler and Ziglio, 1996). According to Helmer (1977) Delphi represents a useful communication device among a group of experts and thus facilitates the formation of a group judgment.[1]

A Delphi process involves carefully selecting experts to serve on the panel. They agree to the purpose and outcome, and also agree to be influenced by their peers.

In our case, nine panelists were identified by a long method of surveying pastors in various areas of North America to determine who was generally perceived to be an expert on pastoral development. The result is the list of names you see in the Acknowledgments section.

Once identified and after they agreed to serve in this capacity, the panelists were asked to write single-statement characteristics of pastoral effectiveness. They did this independently, with no prompting or coaching. They responded with a list of 116 characteristics. These were synthesized to eliminate duplication, and the result was a list of 64 characteristics (see appendix C).

These 64 comprised the instrument used for the consensus-building portion of our effort. The list was sent to each of the panelists and they were asked to rate each characteristic on a Likert scale of 1 to 5 for its importance in describing effectiveness in a pastor.

After each round, the mean score for each characteristic was marked on the instrument and sent another time to the panelists. In this way, they could see the net result of the previous round and how the whole group rated that individual characteristic. This allowed for groupthink to become part of their consideration in the following round.

The panelists received the instrument four times, each with the mean score of the whole group on each characteristic so that they could consider group opinion as they scored each characteristic again. After four times, the mean score was computed and only those with a score of 4.5 or higher were included in the final list of 15. Various panelists noted that all 64 were very important. We agree, but these 15 are of particular importance in light of the expert consensus.

Note

1. David Arditi, "The Delphi Method." http://www.iit.edu/~it/delphi.html (accessed March 2007).

64 SYNTHESIZED CHARACTERISTICS

1. Develops regular habits for spiritual formation (devotions, fasting, solitude)
2. Possesses a lively experience of Gods' grace and growth in his/her Christian walk
3. Is conscious of God's presence in all affairs
4. Demonstrates a thorough understanding and prioritization of the Scriptures
5. Demonstrates through personal actions a genuine concern for the hurting and disenfranchised
6. Demonstrates a concern for missions that results in personal and leadership actions
7. Actively models and leads the congregation in evangelistic outreach to those without Christ
8. Prioritizes and actively leads in ways that build disciples
9. Personally models and leads the congregation in an active pursuit of personal and corporate holiness
10. Possesses a deep, personal love for God
11. Actively demonstrates through leadership actions a love and zeal for the church of Jesus Christ
12. Lives out a clear sense of calling

13. One who not only believes in the power of the Holy Spirit but also expects the Holy Spirit to work in an ongoing way

14. Models an effective, regular, growing prayer life

15. Demonstrates an active engagement in prayer leadership within the congregation, community and Body of Christ.

16. Demonstrates a commitment to the priority of personal and corporate worship

17. Possesses a strong marriage with obvious loving regard for spouse

18. Has godly children in a well-managed household

19. Possesses several deep friendships with people of the same gender

20. Demonstrates the ability to intersect with a wide diversity of people: age, gender, economic and racial

21. Utilizes excellent people skills

22. Able to create an atmosphere of love and respect for people

23. Exhibits a balanced personality that has dealt with any dysfunctions of the past and brought them to resolution (i.e., not likely to panic, become defensive or over-controlling)

24. Possesses a well-developed sense of self-awareness

25. Possesses an attitude of perseverance and tenacity that does not give up easily

26. Demonstrates disciplined work habits

27. Possesses a healthy sense of "drive" exhibited through a willingness to work hard and pursue excellence

28. Consistently demonstrates godly character expressed through manifesting the nine fruits of the Spirit

29. Engages in regular, disciplined study and reading habits

30. Invites and embraces personal accountability

31. Demonstrates an ability to balance priorities

32. Displays an ability to set clear boundaries

33. Exhibits an authentic humility
34. Values and consistently manifests personal integrity
35. Possesses confidence that does not need stroking
36. Demonstrates the ability to make the tough decision
37. Exhibits the ability to take risks
38. Actively demonstrates a godly servant attitude in personal and leadership roles
39. Manifests flexibility to make effective adjustments to ongoing changes
40. Maintains a teachable posture as an eager learner
41. Exhibits a strong desire to grow intellectually (i.e., disciplined study habits—reading, analysis, connections with people who will cause growth)
42. Displays an ability to motivate people to a higher level of individual and corporate life
43. Demonstrates a capability to generate vision
44. Possesses an ability to communicate a vision and motivate others toward it
45. Demonstrates an understanding of human nature
46. Possesses an understanding of what motivates people
47. Possesses an ability to empower other people to lead effectively
48. Possesses an ability to build a strong ministry team
49. Displays an ability to creatively/effectively resolve conflict
50. Demonstrates a willingness to mentor and disciple key leaders
51. Demonstrates an ability to set priorities and adhere to them
52. Demonstrates an ability to manage time effectively
53. Understands and implements a clear strategy for ministry
54. Understands timing for leadership initiatives
55. Demonstrates the ability to act as a change agent, effecting change in people, groups and organizations

56. Possesses the ability to inspire celebration in groups and the church
57. Demonstrates a practical knowledge of how organizations are managed
58. Manifests an ability to effectively teach God's truth in a manner that produces changes in the lives of people
59. Exhibits an ability to preach God's Word in a fresh, invigorating fashion
60. Demonstrates effective communication skills
61. Possesses adequate theological training
62. Is adequately compensated so that distractions are removed
63. Possesses effective cross-cultural skills
64. Manifests a social consciousness through community sensitivity that serves social needs

15 CHARACTERISTICS SUMMARY DESCRIPTIONS

Characteristic 1: Grace and Growth

Effective pastors have a lively experience of God's grace and growth in their Christian walk. They have an ever-increasing realization of their personal need for the daily grace of God in their own lives, and this need motivates them to continually seek personal spiritual development.

Characteristic 2: Love for God

Effective pastors discover and revel in God's passion for them. They prioritize the development of their personal love relationship with God. They see "ministry success" as a cheap imitation of what they really desire: a daily engagement of their heart with God. Without a strong, deep and personal love for God, ministry is in constant danger of devolving into careerism, and ministry as a "job" hobbles the effectiveness of the pastor.

Characteristic 3: Spiritual Formation

Effective pastors recognize their brokenness and consequent need to prepare their souls for the presence of the Holy Spirit through spiritual habits. This vigorous life of spiritual discipline toughens and softens the soul so that daily life is lived from a spiritual center. These disciplines are practices of physical and mental action that give God access to our hearts so that we are shaped to live more like Jesus.

Characteristic 4: Personal Integrity

Effective pastors prioritize the internal and private realms of obedience more than the external, public arena of appearance, and this integrity— the continuity between the internal and external—creates credibility. These pastors are well-formed in the relationship between the bottom and top of their "iceberg." Their actions naturally flow from an identity that is Christlike, whole and integrated into all they do.

Characteristic 5: Love for the Church

Effective pastors are positive and passionate about the nature and mission of the local and global Church, and their love manifests itself in selfless acts of courageous leadership that guide the Church into maturity and outreach. They possess a deep love for the kingdom of God in the world, reflected in the Body of Christ.

Characteristic 6: Servant Leader

Effective pastors approach every relationship with a mind-set of servanthood that asks, "How can I encourage you so that you feel valued and empowered to follow God's destiny for your life?" Their identity is formed as a servant of God fashioned after the mind of Christ. This humility of leadership is bold enough to direct people but is always motivated by God's purposes—not personal gain.

Characteristic 7: Model of Holiness

Effective pastors embrace their influence as a role model of holiness, demonstrating what living like Christ looks like in today's world. They place a priority on helping their congregation be increasingly transformed into Christlike people who bring wholeness to their surroundings.

Characteristic 8: Prayer Life

Effective pastors model a life of effective, regular, growing prayer that is relational at its core, and believe in the power of prayer to influence their lives, the life of the Church and the world around them. This life of prayer permeates all aspects of these pastors' private and public life.

Characteristic 9: Holy Spirit Empowerment

Effective pastors believe in the power of the Holy Spirit. They see themselves as having no power to produce anything of spiritual value without the assistance of the Holy Spirit, and they understand the reality of the spiritual realm and the necessity of spiritual power, operating with a dependency on the Spirit's empowerment and intervention.

Characteristic 10: Inspired Preaching

Effective pastors communicate God's Word in ways that connect truth with the daily questions and needs of people. They grasp equally the condition of the listeners, the creativity of communication and the transforming power of the Scriptures. Inspired preaching is focused, creative, life-giving, rich and connected—to God and to people.

Characteristic 11: Sure Calling

Effective pastors have a deep conviction that their work is an obedient response to God's divine purpose for their lives. They pursue ministry with an urgency, quality and tenacity that portrays God's grip on their souls. Calling is a continuing and dynamic work of God, confirmed by the Church and renewed through the activities of ministry.

Characteristic 12: Godly Character

Effective pastors prioritize the development of their character above the "success" of their church. They demonstrate the life of the Spirit through the characteristics that mark their daily attitudes and actions. Consistent, godly character demonstrated through the manifestation of the fruit of the Spirit is essential for effective pastoral ministry—priority must be placed on roots over results.

Characteristic 13: Personal Accountability

Effective pastors have close friends with whom they share life, friends who are quick to challenge or to affirm the pastor toward godly character and personal excellence. They are vulnerable with others, who give them insight and fuller understanding of their own journey toward effectiveness inwardly and in their leadership.

Characteristic 14: Strong Marriage

Effective pastors prioritize building a marriage that has a life apart from ministry, yet is fortifying to ministry. These pastors cherish, affirm and represent their spouse equally in private and in public. Because marriage finds its source in God, not the civil authorities, and is the place where Kingdom principles should best be seen, effective pastors must evidence a strong marriage—not as a prescriptive formula for ensuring good ministry, but as descriptive evidence that they understand the Kingdom and live its principles in a healthy way at the most obvious and basic level.

Characteristic 15: Visionary Leadership

Effective pastors practice listening to God and collaborating with people to discover a vision for their church. They articulate this vision in public and personal settings in ways that influence people to help bring it into reality. *Having a vision* involves being a ready recipient as well as the means by which the vision comes into focus. *Communicating a vision* deals with how the vision gets shared among the people. *Motivating to a vision* involves how the people are inspired in unity to move toward accomplishing the vision.

ABOUT THE DELPHI PANELISTS

John Burke serves as founding pastor at Gateway Community Church in Austin, Texas, with a focus on the unchurched. He is the author of the book *No Perfect People Allowed*. Before starting Gateway, John was the executive director of ministries at Willow Creek Community Church. Prior to that, John and his wife, Kathy, were on staff with a campus ministry in California. He and Kathy are the parents of two children.

Maxie Dunnam has been a minister in the United Methodist Church since 1955, when at the age of 21, he organized Aldersgate United Methodist Church in Atlanta, Georgia. He served three more congregations before becoming director of the Fellowship Department and then World Editor of *The Upper Room*, the well-known United Methodist publication. In 1982, he became the pastor of Christ United Methodist Church in Memphis, Tennessee. In 1994, he became president of Asbury Theological Seminary and now serves as chancellor. He is an author of many books and continues to be a popular speaker and pastoral resource leader.

Jack Hayford is the founding pastor of The Church On The Way, Van Nuys, California, and the founding president of The King's Seminary. He is a prolific author and serves as the general editor of the Spirit-Filled Life publications. He has composed over 500 hymns, songs and choruses—most notably, the classic "Majesty." Pastor

Jack can be heard around the world on the *Living Way* radio and television program. Currently he serves as president of the International Church of the Foursquare Gospel.

Walter C. Kaiser, Jr. is president emeritus of Gordon-Cornwell Theological Seminary in South Hamilton, Massachusetts. He is the Colman M. Mockler Distinguished Professor of Old Testament and has authored more than 40 books and commentaries. Kaiser is a popular speaker and resource leader for pastors and scholars worldwide and serves on the boards of several Christian organizations.

H.B. London, Jr. is vice president of Ministry Outreach/Pastoral Ministries for Focus on the Family in Colorado Springs, Colorado. A fourth-generation minister, London pastored for 31 years. He also hosted a daily radio program, *Lifeline to Truth*, for 20 years. Since joining the leadership of Focus on the Family, he has directed the development of ministries to pastors and their spouses, and given oversight to ministries affecting physicians, youth culture, the inner city, missionaries, chaplains and basketball camps for the children of single parents in many cities throughout the U.S. and Canada. He has written several books, including *The Heart of a Great Pastor*.

Stephen A. Macchia became the founding president of Leadership Transformations, Inc. (LTi) on July 1, 2003. LTi is a ministry that focuses on the spiritual formation needs of leaders and the spiritual discernment processes of leadership teams in local church and para-church ministry settings nationwide. Formerly, Macchia served for 14 years as president of Vision New England, an association that networked over 5,000 churches. He is author of *Becoming a Healthy Church* and *Becoming a Healthy Disciple.*

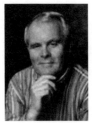

Gordon MacDonald has been a pastor and author for more than 40 years. Presently he serves as editor-at-large for *Leadership Journal* and as chairman of World Relief. His many books include *The Life God Blesses, Renewing Your Spiritual Passion, Rebuilding Your Broken World* and the best-seller, *Ordering Your Private World.* MacDonald can often be found hiking the mountains of New England or Switzerland with his wife, Gail, or their five grandchildren.

Jesse Miranda has a firm commitment to Latino civic engagement. A noted community leader and religious educator for more than 40 years, he served as a pastoral overseer in the Assemblies of God. He is an author and speaker, and currently serves as the director of the Center for Urban Studies and Hispanic Leadership at Vanguard University, and is the president of the *Alianza de Ministerios Evangelicos Nacionales* (AMEN).

Brenda Young serves as pastor of the dynamic and growing Cornerstone Community Church in Akron, Ohio. The church specializes in ministries focused on meeting the current needs of her community. As an influential leader in her denomination, Brenda is a frequent national and international speaker. She serves on several boards, including the National Board for the Free Methodist Church in North America.

God's Word for a Pastor's World

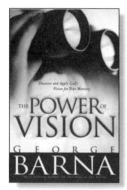

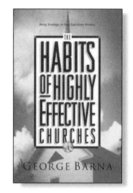
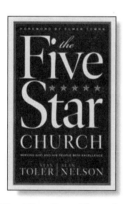

Resources for Pastors

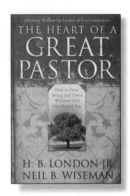
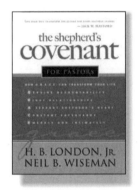

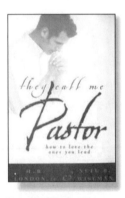